Our Dai...
A Catholic ...

Our Daily Prayer
A Catholic Prayer Book

Dermot Hurley
Society of St Columban, Fiji

author of *Everyday Prayerbook*, etc

Illustrations by
Sister Elizabeth Ruth ODC

COLLINS

Collins Liturgical Publications
8 Grafton Street, London W1X 3LA

Collins Liturgical Australia
Box 316 Blackburn, Victoria 3130

Available in Ireland from
Educational Company of Ireland
21 Talbot Street, Dublin 1

ISBN 0 00 599959 6
© 1986 Dermot Hurley
First published 1987

Nihil obstat: Fr Anton Cowan
Imprimatur: Mgr Ralph Brown VG
Westminster, 3 October 1986
The Nihil obstat and Imprimatur are a declaration that a book or pamphlet is considered to be free from doctrinal or moral error. It is not implied that those who have granted the Nihil obstat and Imprimatur agree with the contents, opinions or statements expressed.

Acknowledgement: Psalm texts are from *The Psalms: a new translation* © copyright 1963 The Grail (England), published by Collins. Used by permission.

Typeset by Bookmag, Henderson Road, Inverness
Printed in Great Britain by William Collins, Glasgow

Contents

Foreword *by* Cardinal Manning — 7

Preface — 8

Introduction
Praying — 9
Outline of the Book — 10
When and How to Pray — 12
Additional Notes — 14

The Presence of God — 17

Living with Jesus, in the Father, by the Spirit — 24
1001 Prayers — 32

Praying from the New Testament
Introduction — 37
Life of Jesus from the Gospels — 43
Holy Spirit sent by Father and Son — 48

Praying with God's People
Psalms of David — 52
People of the Gospel — 68
Responding to Jesus' Last Supper talk — 71
Responding to Epistles — 80
Prayers of Saints — 89

The Blessed Eucharist
Reflections — 97
Prayers before Mass — 107
Prayers before Communion — 113
Prayers after Communion or after Mass — 120
Prayers before the Blessed Sacrament — 128

The Sacrament of Reconciliation
Introduction — 143
Readings for Confession — 144
Prayers before Confession — 150
Prayers after Confession — 159

The Sacrament of Marriage
Prayers for Married Couples — 166

Devotion to Our Lady
Introduction — 175
Praying the Mysteries of the Rosary — 175
The Joyful Mysteries — 180
The Sorrowful Mysteries — 183
The Glorious Mysteries — 186

Marian Devotions for Today
Novena to Our Lady, Mother of the Church — 189
 I. We honour and love her — 191
 II. We call on her for help — 197
 III. We promise to imitate her — 201

The Communion of Saints
Reflection on the Saints — 203
Litany of the Saints — 208

Reflections on death
Purgatory — 213
Prayers — 215

Index — 219

Foreword

The author and compiler of this book of prayers is a holy man. From the cradle on he and his two brother priests, and a distinguished religious sister, were nourished in faith and devotion. Their home was in truth a domestic church. Little wonder then that in far off Fiji ripples of that context should surround the simple people of God's household.

We admire the zeal of this missionary priest. We hope that his lessons on prayer will be effective sources of holiness for his flock. The volume is an answer, surely, to the root question of all the followers of the Lord — 'Teach us how to pray'.

Timothy, Cardinal Manning
Retired Archbishop of Los Angeles

Preface

This is not a book to be read from cover to cover at one sitting, but rather a handbook, to be used at times of prayer. It offers a variety of methods and suggestions to help people make better use of the different prayer-moments of their lives, and those using it will find different sections useful at different times.

I have spent more than thirty years in pastoral work in Fiji, and this book grew out of actual parish situations and needs. It is composed of material originally prepared as various pamphlets to help parishioners use more fully the opportunities they found in their lives for personal, family, group and sacramental prayer.

As English was a second language for most of the people, I tried to use simple and direct English in putting before them deep and adult spiritual approaches to God. But because God is one term of the relationship of prayer, I have always been conscious of our human limitations, for no human words, whether simple or difficult, whether everyday or theological, can ever fully express the reality that is experienced in prayer by people called and led into the mystery of God's inner life by Jesus Christ.

Much of the material was prepared for people beginning their prayer-life. But I hope others with more prayer-experience will also find it useful — as I myself do. For, in spite of having been praying in one way or another for sixty years, I often find that the material presented here can stimulate me to prayer when I am so busy or distracted that prayer is difficult. But I remind all users, whether beginners or experienced, that the value of their prayer will depend, under God's love which is always with them, far more on their own personal efforts than on the words of this book.

Dermot Hurley
May 1986

Introduction

PRAYING

A human act of mind and will

Of all God's creatures in this world only people are able to pray. Unlike animals, they know who they are, they can think and love, they are made in God's image and likeness — and they can pray.

In praying we raise our minds and hearts to God — and we are enabled to reach him only through his gifts of faith, hope and charity which are available for our use whenever we sincerely turn to God. But it remains our duty as well as our privilege to learn how to use our human powers more effectively in prayer.

For the minds which we use to make praying a uniquely human action are dependent on our senses, by which we immediately perceive the world we live in. What we see, hear and feel — and what we remember and imagine — can so absorb us that we often find it difficult to turn to God, whom we cannot directly see or hear or feel. We need therefore to seek (and to use) help to learn how to pray better — and especially to learn how to use human words to express and to foster the prayer-thoughts and prayer-desires of our soul.

Learning a skill

Like reading, driving a car or playing a game, praying is a skill. To do it well, we must be willing to find time for effective training. To train for the skill to play a game well we must first learn the purpose and rules of the game. Then, to help our mind and muscles act effectively, we learn exercises which we repeat and practise regularly. Only then can we hope to start playing the game well — and each time we play, we use and improve our skill.

Exercises of prayer

Prayer is a very personal thing. Each person prays in his or her individual and unique way. But we can not pray without first learning to pray, which means we must start by being taught by others, especially by people very close to God who have shown us the many different ways they prayed.

We can read their prayers, using the words they used and making them our own as we repeat them in our prayers to God. Prayerbooks with collections of prayers of saints and other holy people are therefore a very reliable way of enabling us to learn and practise praying.

OUTLINE OF THE BOOK

The presence of God

The first section of this book offers exercises to help us raise our minds to God, and keep it fixed on him, as we turn to him and try to open our lives to him in thoughts and words. This section looks on God as our creator, who made us because he loves us. Recognizing him as the reason and source of our lives is the essential basis for all real religion — and for all real prayer.

The Psalms

This sense of the presence of God is most obvious in the Psalms. In selecting psalms for this book, the main criteria was their value as prayer. All those chosen are addressed directly TO God, and omitted are those which speak about God, or exhort his people — as well as those with pre-Christian theology and those based narrowly on Jewish history or geography.

But even though in the work of creation, as in all works outside himself, God works as the one and only God, we know, through our faith in Christ's teaching, that in that one God there are three divine persons, really distinct from each other as they live and relate to one another in the inner, hidden life of God.

Living with Jesus, in the Father, by the Spirit

The next section therefore helps us to enter, so to speak, into the mystery of life of the Trinity through our union with Christ — a union which is his free gift.

Through our union with Jesus Christ, the second person of the Trinity who became man, we can become adopted sons of God the Father, and in some way as the Son does, we can pray and relate to the Father and Holy Spirit as distinct persons *within* the very nature and being of God.

This section includes short readings and prayer exercises intended to help us appreciate and strengthen our union with Christ, and go more easily and more effectively with him and through him to his Father, and be more receptive to the gift of the Holy Spirit whom the Father sends for our work in this world, as he sent him to Jesus and the apostles in this same world 2,000 years ago . . .

These exercises and the '1001 prayer-sets' that follow them, can help us to basic mental prayer, through the use of short prayer formulas, which we should first use as indicated so as to learn which of them are more relevant and useful for us to continue in the future.

Outline of the Book

Praying from the New Testament

The next section suggests ways of using the New Testament for prayer, and especially of using, while reading Gospels or Epistles, the prayer-formulas of previous sections. Also included are selections of New Testament passages suitable for prayer, listed under headings which will help people identify and find passages that relate to their needs.

Praying with God's people

Here prayers are built up from New Testament passages, taking concepts and words used about God and addressing them to him as prayer, with occasional additions to make the prayer relevant to our needs today.

Here too are prayers actually used by the saints of later centuries, showing us how they approached God in prayer.

All these can be used at any time. When we become familiar with what is offered we can easily choose suitable prayer formulas for the times and opportunities that we find in our day to day living — such times as morning and night prayer, prayers during sickness (our own, or that of others), prayers on the occasion of a death, a funeral etc.

Such prayer opportunities are very personal, indeed unique, so we should accept the freedom to choose our own prayers for such occasions rather than limiting ourselves to prayers chosen by someone else.

Sacramental occasions: Eucharist, Reconciliation, Marriage

Separate sections contain readings and prayers prepared to help make our Confessions, Masses and Visits to the Blessed Sacrament more valuable. We all make use of these sacramental actions at certain times, and suitably chosen prayers can make these occasions more valuable and rewarding. Also included are some prayers for married couples, based largely on liturgical and other church writings, to help them live the commitments of their marriage sacrament in their daily lives.

Praying to Our Lady and the saints

The section on the rosary offers some new suggestions to help us deepen our prayer on the mysteries of the rosary. A Marian novena based on the key concepts of the Constitution on the Church of the Second Vatican Council, which presents the church's teaching on Our Lady, is given.

Then comes a section explaining why and how praying to the saints fits into our worship of God, why we pray to them, seek their help and try to imitate them. An expanded version of the traditional litany of the saints follows. A reflection on death and purgatory with accompanying prayers concludes the book.

WHEN AND HOW TO PRAY

When to pray

Jesus told us we should always pray, and we can try to do so by living our daily lives with our minds basically fixed on him and his Father in heaven, and with the basic intention of pleasing him in everything we do.

But we live in a world whose distractions are close and constant, and whose attractions are persuasively presented in the mass media of everyday life. We will not even be able to begin to 'pray always' in this sense, unless we deliberately and seriously seek and set aside some definite occasions for keeping our minds fixed on God, and giving our whole selves to him for appreciable periods of time.

Traditionally, we have been advised and led to pray each morning and night, but many find other opportunities for prayer — times deliberately set aside from our usual routine — retreats, holy hours, prayer-meetings etc. — or opportunities used as they occur — sickness, sleeplessness, wakes, funerals — and travel, with its opportunities for shared prayer (especially perhaps the Rosary) if we travel with family or friends, and opportunities for personal meditative prayer if we travel alone.

Bodily posture

In our efforts to 'pray always' we must be ready to pray in whatever posture we find outselves — driving, walking, sitting, standing etc., etc.

But at the times we deliberately set aside for praying in the strict sense, we should each choose and seek the posture which is most suitable for us — and we should not be afraid to change it occasionally.

Praying is an act of our soul, and our soul is the principle of life for our body as well as for our mind and will. So *we* can 'pray' also with our body, and should learn to do so, and choose the actions most helpful to us each particular time we pray.

Some find the traditional posture of kneeling most helpful, as a sign of lowering ourselves in love before God, our maker. Others will sit comfortably, so that the body will not obtrude itself on their consciousness as they turn their mind to God. Some will pray better standing up, or in some yoga position, while others will find prayer easier as they walk, especially in familiar and quiet surroundings — and some can even use their footsteps to beat out the rhythm of a rhythmic prayer or hymn.

Others find it useful to pace their prayer to their breathing, and I am very grateful to Fr. Di Mello's excellent book *Sadhana*, from which I have adapted some of the breathing and prayer exercises in the early part of this book.

Bodily actions

Some will join their hands in the traditional way while praying, as a spire pointing their whole being towards God and focussing their attention and life on him. Others will clasp their hands before them, as a sign of uniting their whole being and actions as they turn to God. Others will raise their hands as a sign of raising their souls and whole lives to God.

Some will close their eyes so as to shut out the world and its distractions. Others will kneel or sit with downcast eyes, as a sign of accepting their inability to see God whom they are addressing. Some will open their eyes to look on the tabernacle, or on a crucifix, or on some beauty of God's creation, or on anything else that helps them to focus their mind on things of God. Genuflecting and bowing are signs of worship, striking the breast is a sign of sorrow, and the sign of the cross reminds us of Calvary.

All such postures and actions can become real prayers if we deliberately try to bring our body as well as our soul to our prayer. But they can also become routine through habit, and thus often meaningless as prayer, which to be a human action demands that we know and deliberately choose what we are doing. So we should often examine our posture and actions, recall their meaning and usefulness, and change them if we find others more helpful.

Silences

Silence can also help us to pray, just as outside noises can distract us from God. But silence can also become a prayer in itself. As mentioned elsewhere short silences can be achieved by pausing at the end of the lines or sentences we read. These will allow us to dwell attentively and lovingly on God, to whom the words of our prayer have been addressed, or about whom the words of scripture have been written.

Other times can also be deliberately set aside for silences, but more often they will occur naturally, as a part of our prayer, and should be so used without fear, or without feeling that we have to finish or 'make up for' the rest of the prayers we planned to use, but perhaps omitted because of such silence. But even if we do not at times make such silences in our times set aside for prayer, we can discover many periods of 'silences' in our lives, and use them well for prayer — helped perhaps by using some verse or phrase from prayers we have memorized, and which can sum up at that time our basic reaching out to God.

Short mental prayers and desires of this kind will sanctify our silences, and will also sanctify whatever activity follows. And in time they can easily and naturally lead to the deeper silence of prayer and love, as we turn our minds to God and merely 'attend' to him and his love without words as a mother 'attends' to her child while silently sitting with him.

ADDITIONAL NOTES

Overlapping

Readers will find some over-lapping, with certain ideas, and even words, repeated in different prayers — and this should not surprise them. For certain approaches and themes are basic to our prayer, and we tend to return to them again and again in different and varying circumstances of our life. This is similiar to the repetition we find in the 150 psalms of the Old Testament, and in the prayers of Christ and his apostles, which return again and again to loving God and our neighbour through acts of faith, hope and charity, and to a comparison of this world and the next, and to the warnings against the sinfulness that keeps us from God.

'I' and 'We'

All the prayers are addressed *to* God. None are addressed to others; none are written in the third person about others, and none are written in the third person as words of praise about God. Each prayer therefore is written in the first person, some in the singular and some in the plural according to what was thought suitable at the time of preparing each particular prayer.

However a prayer in plural form may sometimes be more relevant to *your* personal needs when you are praying alone, and then you can easily change the 'we' and 'us' to 'I' and 'me' as you read.

Prayers in the singular are of course more appropriate when you are praying by yourself, and for your own particular needs and situation. But even then it is well to remember that you are never really 'alone' when you are praying. You are always a member of the Church, united through Christ to other members of his body, and your 'I' always at least implicitly can mean 'I and the Church', or 'and some other', for whom you wish to pray.

This is particularly true of the Psalms, many of which, though written in the first person singular, can be more effectively used in the name of the Church, as priests and religious do when they pray the Divine Office. It is usually enough to remember this as we read; but if we are using a prayer with others, or reading it aloud for others, we may prefer to substitute 'we' for 'I' and 'us' for 'me' as we read . . .

We should remember the little words 'we' and 'us' are among the most important in our prayers. When praying alone, it is good occasionally to pause after using them, and to recall explicitly and positively all those we want to pray for, or to bring with ourselves before God — particularly the world or the Church as a whole, or particular groups, family, friends or enemies, the poor or neglected, the sick or the suffering, politicians or church leaders etc., and even make the pause long enough for us to pronounce their names to ourselves.

Sense lines

Many of the prayers are written in 'sense lines' to encourage more frequent pauses as we read. When we are praying privately, such pauses can be prolonged to give ample opportunity for us to think quietly of the meaning of the phrases we have read, or perhaps to draw in a breath as we repeat some short prayer or mantra from the early part of this book — or even to repeat the line a second time, or even more often!

If we are leading a group in prayer by reading the prayer for them, each pause will enable others to dwell a little on the phrase they have heard, or even to repeat it silently (or perhaps aloud if desired). While if people are reading the prayer together, the pause at the end of each sense-line will help them stay together with less distractions from one another.

Rhythmic prayer

Many of the prayers have been presented in a rhythmic version — but unrhymed to allow the thoughts to be more clearly, simply and directly expressed than if a rhyme were sought.

The rhythm will make memorising easier, and will enable many such prayers to be sung as hymns if desired. Sometimes a suitable and well known tune for the rhythm is suggested, or the line-metre indicated to help a suitable tune to be selected. Hymns are prayers set to music, and St Augustine said that he prays twice who sings his prayer.

Even when alone, singing a verse or two, or singing each line or couple of lines a few times in a quiet song to yourself, or 'humming' it silently under your breath, can help you fix your mind more effectively on what you are praying.

Even without singing, and in non-rhythmic prayers, it is also good to repeat lines, phrases, or sentences a few times, and sometimes to say them aloud and so to use more of your body than if you used your eyes alone to read them.

The Presence of God

Preliminary breathing exercise

Breathing is a sign of life. The air I breathe keeps each part of my body alive. While I live, even when I am sleeping, or unconscious, I am breathing. I stop breathing only when I die. As long as I am still breathing, I am alive. Yet I usually take it for granted, and seldom think of it. Breathing is one of God's greatest gifts to me, and it is therefore good for me sometimes to observe it and notice it. This is something I can learn to do in this first breathing exercise. Some find it useful to do this or the next exercise for a few moments before starting later exercises and prayers in this handbook, or indeed before starting any period of prayer.

> I observe my breathing: in... out... in... out...
> I draw air in... I push it out... in... out...
> I leave it as it is... I do not change it...
> I just notice it as it is... deep or shallow...
> I feel it touching my nostrils... hot or cold...
> Where do I feel it most?... nose? throat? lungs?
> Do I feel it more coming in?... or going out?...
> I remain conscious of how it feels... in... out...
> Quietly, without strain, I continue doing this...
>
> I take note of my breathing for 2-3 minutes...
> When my mind wanders... I start again...
> I return my attention to my breathing... in... out...

God formed man of dust from the ground, and breathed into his nostrils the breath of life, and man became a living being. (Gen 2:7)

God fashioned the earth and all that lives there; he gave life and breath to all its people. (Isaiah in Is 42:5)

I will give you sinews and muscles and cover you with skin. I will put breath into you and bring you back to life.
(God's message to the dry bones in Ez 37:6)

It is God himself who gives life and breath and everything else to everyone. (St Paul in Acts 17:25)

God everywhere, God here!

>Air enables all people, all living creatures, to live.
>God made the air, and the lungs I breathe it with.
>By my breathing he keeps me alive and enables me to act.
>God's power created me, and the air to keep me alive.
>God knows all things: he knows the air I breathe.
>God is everywhere: he is in the air I am now breathing.
>The air I breathe is not God, but his loving gift to me.
>It is an ever-present sign of all his other gifts to me.

You created every part of me; you put me together in my mother's womb ... When my bones were being formed, carefully put together in my mother's womb, when I was growing there in secret, you know that I was there — you saw me before I was born. (David in Ps 138:13-14)

God looked at everything he had made and he was very pleased.
(Gen 1:31)

For all things exist through him and for him. To God be the glory forever. Amen. St Paul in Rom 11:36)

Remember that you made me from clay; you formed my body with bones and sinews and covered the bones with muscles and skin. You have given me life and constant love, and your care has kept me alive.
(Job in Job 8:9-12)

Ever since God created the world, his invisible qualities, both his eternal power and his divine nature have been clearly seen; they are perceived in the things that God has made. . . .
(St Paul in Rom 1:20)

>I can remember God's presence as I observe my breathing.
>As I breathe in, I think of God, while praying the first part.
>As I breathe out I pray the next part, thinking of myself.
>I repeat each line a few times, or until I am distracted.
>I insert my name after each 'I' below:—

BREATHING IN BREATHING OUT

God is in the air I draw in . . . . I breathe it out.
God keeps me alive by his air . . . . I am a living person.
God's wisdom planned this air . . . . he formed me to use it.
God's strength is in the air . . . . I live by his power.
God cares for me in his air . . . . I need his loving care.
God loves me for he is good . . . . I love God for I need him.
God can live without me . . . . . . I cannot live without God.

The Presence of God

God in me

God is everywhere — in all living and non-living things.
He is present in a special unique way in living people.
We have minds and wills, and we can know and love God.
Only *people* can know the presence of God who is in them.
We know that he who chose and made us, wants to live in us.
We pray when we respond to our loving God present in us.
He lives in us; we should want to live in him and for him.

No one has ever seen God, but as long as we love one another, God will live in us. (St John in 1 Jn 4:13)

Whoever keeps God's commandments lives in God and God in him. (St John in 1 Jn 3:24)

God is not far from any of us, since it is in him that we live, and move, and exist. (St Paul in Acts 17:28)

I pray that God will make his home in your hearts through faith. (St Paul in Eph 3:17)

Surely you know that you are God's temple, and that God's Spirit lives in you. (St Paul in 1 Cor 3:16)

God is love, and whoever lives in love, lives in union with God and God lives in union with him. (St John in 1 Jn 4:16)

I chose you before I gave you life, and before you were born, I selected you to be a prophet to the nations. (God in Jer 1:4)

I pray

BREATHING IN	BREATHING OUT
I breathe your air	I'm still alive.
In all you made	I find you, Lord.
I rest in you	God everywhere.
Lord, come to me	I turn to you.
Lord, stay with me	I cling to you.
Come, rest in me	and give me peace.
I keep your law	to live in you.
I live in you	I live in love.
And in your love	I love your friends.
You live in me	I live in you.
Come, make your home	within my heart.
Within my soul	abide in me.

My creator's presence

BREATHING IN	BREATHING OUT

You made my lungs .... to breathe your air.
I breathe your air .... I'm still alive!
Alive and well .... I thank you, Lord.
In thanks and love .... I'll live for you.

Creator God .... you made all things.
You made all things........ and keep them made.
In all you made .... you show yourself.
And I can find .... you anywhere.

You're present, Lord .... in all you made.
In all I see .... I search for you.
Your wisdom, care .... and power I find.
I rest in you .... God, everywhere.

God everywhere .... in all you made.
My soul you made .... to be like you.
Made like to you .... I know and love.
I know you live .... within my soul.

Now present, Lord .... within my soul,
Abide in me .... and make us one.
Made one with you .... I live in you.
I live in you .... and love you, Lord.

You gave me life .... to live for you.
You made my mind .... to know your plan.
You made my will .... so I could love.
You made my hands .... to work for you.

My Father's care

BREATHING IN	BREATHING OUT

Creator God, ... you made me well.
You made me, 'me' .... I am your choice.
You chose me, Lord .... to live for you.
The life you gave .... I use in love.

With Father's love .... you formed my life,
and forming me .... made me your child.
Your chosen child .... I need your love.
Your love alone .... can fill my life.

To love you, Lord, ... I do your will;
but I am weak .... and need your help.
Come, strengthen me .... each day I live.
Each day I live .... Lord, stay with me.

Come, stay with me .... till end of day.
Each hour today .... I need your care.
Come, show your love .... and teach me, Lord,
to love all those .... you made and love.

You made and sent .... all those I meet,
all chosen, called .... and loved like me.
You loved them first .... I love them too.
I love you, Lord, ... in those I meet.

In those I meet .... I seek you, Lord:
in parents, spouse, ... in children, friends.
In those I hurt .... or who hurt me:
'Forgive us, Lord .... as we forgive'.

Our Daily Prayer

An act of love   (based on Mark 12:29-31)

BREATHING IN	BREATHING OUT

I love you, Lord . . . . with all my heart;
with all my heart . . . . and all my soul;
with all my soul . . . . and all my mind,
with all my mind . . . . and all my strength.

I love you, Lord . . . . with all my heart —
My heart is mine . . . . alone to give.
I give my heart . . . . to you alone.
From sinful loves, ... I turn to you.

I love you, Lord . . . . with all my soul,
with soul and life, ... in all I do.
In all I do, ... each hour I live.
your gift of life . . . . I'll use for you.

I love you, Lord . . . . with all my mind.
You made my mind . . . . to know your truth.
Your truth and life . . . . show me your way.
I know your way . . . . and do your will.

I love you, Lord . . . . with all my strength:
But I am weak . . . . and often fail.
Forgive me now . . . . I need your help.
Come, help me, Lord . . . . I trust in you.

I love you, Lord . . . . who first loved me.
You gave me life . . . . I am your choice.
You chose me, Lord . . . . to know and love.
I use your gifts . . . . to work for you.

I love you, Lord . . . . and all your friends,
for you chose them . . . . as you chose me.
As you love me . . . . I love them, Lord.
I love them all . . . . for they are yours.

Living with Jesus, in the Father, by the Spirit

Through, with and in Jesus

God wants to share his life with each person he made,
For this God the Son became man, sent by God the Father.
In God's plan, Jesus his Son first unites us with himself,
through his new life, which he gives us in baptism.
Without his gift, we have no way of being one with him.
Holy Communion is the outward 'sign' of this union.
The bible describes our union with Jesus in these words:

Abide in me and I in you. As the branch cannot bear fruit of itself unless it abide in the vine, so neither can you unless you abide in me. He who abides in me and I in him bears much fruit, for without me you can do nothing. (Jesus in Jn 15:4-5)

He who eats my flesh and drinks my blood lives in me, and I live in him. (Jesus in Jn 6:56)

It is no longer I who live, but it is Christ who lives in me.
(St Paul in Gal 2:20)

Surely you know that Christ Jesus is in you. (St Paul in 2 Cor 13:5)

God has given us eternal life and this life has its source in the Son. Whoever has the Son has this life. (St John in 1 Jn 5:11)

It is through faith that all of you are God's sons in union with Christ Jesus. You were baptised into union with Christ. (St Paul in Gal 3:26-27)

I am the way, the truth and the life; no one goes to the Father except through me. (Jesus in Jn 14:6)

I pray to Jesus

BREATHING IN	BREATHING OUT
Christ, come to me	and live in me.
Christ, live in me	I live in you.
Abide in me	and make us one.
Give me your life	to love like you.
With your new life	I'm born again.
Made one with you	I live your life.
Christ, living bread	to feed my soul.
Christ, food divine	come strengthen me.
Come, bread from heav'n	to lead me home.
You are the Word	made flesh for me.
The Word of God	you make him known.
You share God's life	and share mine too.
My Lord, my God	I worship you.
You died for me	I live for you.
You suffered pain	I offer mine.
Christ, sent by God	I'm sent by you.
Christ, sent in love	send me to love.
Good shepherd, Christ	take care of me.
You call me friend	I long for you.
My friend unseen	I seek your face.
My hands in yours	I seek my God.
You are the Way	to guide me home.
You are the Truth	to fill my mind.
You are the Life	through you I live.
Christ, fill my heart	I thirst for you.
When tired I come	you give me rest.
Your yoke is sweet	your burden light.
You want my life	to work for you.
You want my heart	to love your friends.
You want my mind	to plan for you.
You want my hands	to work for you.

The Jesus Prayer (adapted)

The name of Jesus is the basis of this prayer. In its traditional form, the phrase, 'Lord Jesus Christ, have mercy on me' is repeated again and again. In this adaptation, other rhythmic phrases have been added, to enable us to vary our prayer.

BREATHING IN	BREATHING OUT
Lord Jesus Christ	be merciful.
Lord Jesus Christ	forgive my sins.
Lord Jesus Christ	I need your love.
Lord Jesus Christ	I long for you.
Lord Jesus Christ	make me your friend.
Lord Jesus Christ	make me your joy.
Lord Jesus Christ	remember me.
Lord Jesus Christ	I seek your help.
Lord Jesus Christ	I trust in you.
Lord Jesus Christ	I praise your name.
Lord Jesus Christ	I worship you.
Lord Jesus Christ	I give you thanks.
Lord Jesus Christ	I know your will.
Lord Jesus Christ	I love your plan.
Lord Jesus Christ	come, live in me.
Lord Jesus Christ	I follow you.
Lord Jesus Christ	I want to serve.
Lord Jesus Christ	come, heal and save.
Lord Jesus Christ	you are my way.
Lord Jesus Christ	you are my truth.
Lord Jesus Christ	you are my life.

Daily Offering

My mind on you	Lord Jesus Christ.
My heart for you	Lord Jesus Christ.
My life with you	Lord Jesus Christ.
My soul in you	Lord Jesus Christ.
My strength from you	Lord Jesus Christ.
My joy through you	Lord Jesus Christ.

Living with Jesus, in the Father, by the Spirit

The Name of Jesus

When we grow to know Jesus well, we get so familiar with him that calling on his name is in itself a prayer. The name, 'Jesus' means 'Saviour' — 'he who saves', or 'he who heals'. When we use his name as a call for help, he answers as he did during his life on earth, and can heal our illness — physical, mental, emotional and above all spiritual. He forgives our sins and brings us peace with God, with our fellow men and with ourselves.

I remember Jesus in his words and actions in the Gospels, or in the Stations, or in Rosary Mysteries, and I recall that the same Jesus is in me now, and I ask him to touch and live in each part of my soul and body to heal and strengthen me . . . And I recall that he wants others to find him in me, as he wants me to find him in them, and I ask him to touch and heal my friends.

I SLOWLY CALL ON THE NAME	I RECALL IN TURN AND SEPARATELY
JESUS	each faculty of my soul: mind, will, imagination, memory, each feeling that I recognise.
JESUS	each of my senses: sight, hearing, smell, touch, taste.
JESUS	each part of my body: hands, feet, eyes, ears, heart, etc.
JESUS	each spiritual weakness and vice: my pride, my greed, my laziness, my impurity, my envy, my unkindness, my anger, my vanity, my gluttony.
JESUS	each virtue I try to practise: faith, hope, charity, service, kindness, humility, worship, prudence, honesty, purity, obedience, etc.
JESUS	my friends... members of my family... my opponents... my enemies...
JESUS	groups that need my prayers: the sick, those in prison, refugees, sinners, poor, blind, deaf, other Christians, non-Christians.
JESUS	people I will meet today: at work, at home, travelling, at games.

The Sacred Heart of Jesus

The human heart is for all races the sign and seat of love.
Jesus is true man — with a human heart like ours.
His heart is the sign and seat of his human love for us.
Like ours, it beats faster in joy and slower in sorrow.

This human heart belongs to a divine person, God the Son.
Jesus is the Second Person of the Trinity who became man.
He is united in the Trinity with his Father and the Spirit.
We can adore his heart for it belongs to a divine person.
United with Father and Son in heaven, Jesus is still man.
His heart is still part of his risen and glorious body.
It can now be the sign of his infinite divine love for us.
We call his heart 'sacred' and address prayers to it.
Praying to his Sacred Heart, we are calling on his love.
His love for us is human — but also divine and infinite.

I picture Jesus in some event of his life,
and address him by repeating the first phrase each time:

O SACRED HEART OF JESUS CHRIST

— be merciful to me.
— in love forgive my sins.
— come, make my heart like yours.
— I place my trust in you.
— be thou my peace and joy.
— I try to give you joy.
— come, form yourself in me.
— pour out your love on me.
— I work to make you loved.
— I know your love for me.
— you burn with love for me.
— I offer you my thanks.
— I want to make you glad.
— help me to love like you.
— I trust your love for me.

God, my Father, through Jesus

Jesus is God's Son by the divine nature they both possess.
With the Holy Spirit, they share the inner life of God.

As creatures, we stand outside God to honour our creator.
Jesus wants us to share the inner life of the Trinity.
With him, we can enter the personal life of the Trinity.
United to him, we become adopted children of the Father,
and we receive his Spirit, whom he sends to guide us.
Through Jesus, we, creatures, can love God as our Father.

We cannot understand this mystery by reading or study.
But we believe it, and can live it in our prayer.
With Jesus our brother, we call God 'Father' like he does.
We should always try to pray the 'Our Father' as he did.
The bible expresses this mystery in our human language:

'In a little while the world will see me no more, but you will see me, and because I live, you also will live. When that day comes, you will know that I am in my Father and that you are in me, just as I am in you.'
(Jesus in Jn 14:19-20)

'I pray that they may all be one, Father. May they be in us, just as you are in me, and I am in you. I gave them the same glory you gave me, so that they may be one, just as you and I are one: I in them, and you in me, so that they may be completely one.' (Jesus in Jn 17:21-23)

Christ has given us the very great gifts he promised . . . so that you may come to share God's nature.' (St Peter in 2 Pet 1:4)

Those whom God has already chosen, he set apart to become like his Son so that the Son would become first among many brothers. And those whom God set apart, he called, and those he called, he put right with himself, and shared his glory with them. (St Paul in Rom 8:29-30)

'The Father's love is so great that we are called God's children — and so in fact we are. My dear friends, we are now God's children but it is not yet clear what we shall become. But we know that when Christ appears, we shall be like him, for we shall see him as he really is. (St John in 1 Jn 3:1-3)

Because of his love, God had already decided that through Jesus Christ he would make us his sons — this was his pleasure and purpose.
(St Paul in Eph 1:4-5)

BREATHING IN	BREATHING OUT

Christ's Father, God .... my Father too.
My brother, Christ .... makes me your child.
I am your child .... my Father, God.

Christ lives in me .... I live in him.
I live in Christ .... he lives in you.
Made one with Christ .... I live in you.

Christ lives in me .... to love in me.
Christ loves you, Lord .... I love with him.
In Christ I love .... you, Father, God.

Through Christ your Son .. you formed my being.
With Christ your Son .... in you I live.
In Christ your Son .... I work for you.

Through Christ your Son ...... I know your truth.
With Christ your Son .... I choose your will.
In Christ your Son .... I serve your friends.

Through Christ my Way .... I find you, Lord.
With Christ my Truth .... I know your plan.
In Christ my Life .... I live in you.

You made me, Lord .... I am your choice.
You formed my life .... with Father's love.
With Father's love .... you care for me.
Take care of me .... I need your love.

With Christ I love .... my Father, God.
With Christ I pray .... your name be praised.
With Christ I long .... your kingdom come.
With Christ I thirst .... your will be done.

With Christ I beg .... give bread to all.
With Christ I plead .... forgive our sins.
With Christ I cry .... remove our trials.
With Christ I call .... from evil save.

Living with Jesus, in the Father, by the Spirit

God, Spirit of love, sent by Father and Son

In God's inner life, the Father and Son love one another.
The inner love is a third Person, called the Holy Spirit.
He shares God's full life in all actions outside God.
Within God, he is a person distinct from Father and Son.
He is also a distinct person to us who share God's life.
One with Jesus, we share in his relation with the Spirit.
When I love the Father with Jesus, the Spirit is with me.
He guided Jesus in becoming man and in his life on earth.
So, he is sent to guide and teach us in our lives here.
The bible expresses this mystery in our human language:

The Helper, the Holy Spirit, whom the Father will send in my name, will teach you everything and make you remember all that I have told you. (Jesus in Jn 14:26)

By the Spirit's power we cry out to God, 'Father, my Father!' God's Spirit joins himself to our spirits to declare that we are God's children.
(St Paul in Rom 8:15)

No one can confess 'Jesus is Lord,' unless he is guided by the Holy Spirit. (St Paul in 1 Cor 12:3)

There are different kinds of spiritual gifts, but the same Spirit gives them. (St Paul in 1 Cor 12:4)

When the Spirit comes, who reveals the truth about God, he will lead you into all the truth. (Jesus in John 16:13)

```
Come, Spirit of Christ........    make me like him.
Come, Spirit of God..............  and fill my life.
Come, Spirit of Strength  ......  protect the weak.
Come, Spirit of Love    ......   and cleanse my soul.
Come, Spirit of Truth ............  direct my mind.
Come, Holy Spirit................    make me holy.
Come, Spirit of Life..............   and live in me.
Come, Spirit of Joy ..........    give faith and love.
Come, Spirit of Peace ........    renew God's world.
Come, Spirit of Hope  ........    help me trust God.
Come, Holy Spirit...............   and fill my heart.
Come, Spirit All-wise  ........   help me know God.
Come, Spirit of Faith  ....  proclaim Christ's words.
Come, Spirit of Light ............  shine out in me.
```

1001 PRAYERS

Explanation

Jesus reminded us that God cares for us, and that to love God is our most important human duty, on which all religious practices should be based. In prayer I fulfill this duty in words like 'I love you, my God'.

Such words will have different meanings at different times, because I change at each moment of my life, and so do my needs, hopes, desires, etc. God does not change, but my human mind cannot grasp him as he is in himself and therefore, each time I pray, I find myself limited to one or other of his revealed attributes or titles. Also the relationship between God and me can at times be more fittingly expressed by verbs other than 'love' or 'forgive'.

The following 'prayer-sets' are based on such variations. By choosing one phrase from each of the three columns listed in each set, I can build up a prayer suitable for my particular needs from the 1,001 possible combinations of each set. The rhythm will help me to memorize them for use during the day, or to fit them into some regular bodily rhythm like walking, breathing etc., or to sing or hum them to suitable tunes.

For personal prayer (preferably after reading a little of the New Testament): after reading the chosen prayer a few times, close your eyes, and repeat it silently in your mind, thinking of the meaning of the words for you, and keeping your heart fixed on God and his love.

For group prayer: the leader, reads a chosen 3-phrase prayer aloud, changing 'I' to 'we' as desired. The others repeat it a few times, first aloud and then silently, for a period that may be ended by the group being led in singing it to some familiar tune.

To pray for others: use the plural 'we-form' instead of the singular 'I-form', remembering the person or people we wish to pray for as we do so . . . or inserting their names, using the third person where needed.

1,001 Jesus prayers

(Lord) Jesus (repeated before each prayer)

Christ, true Son of God,	**come, pardon me,**	I turn from sin.
Word of God made flesh,		I turn to you.
Christ, my Lord and God,	**take care of me,**	I trust in you.
		I know your love.
fruit of Mary's womb,	**increase my faith,**	my flesh is weak.
choosing me as friend,		and make me good.
Christ, Redeemer, King,	**come, live in me,**	and keep me pure.
who died for us,		I thirst for you.
risen from the dead,	**come, strengthen me,**	I seek your help.
bread of life for us,		I need your love.
offering Mass with us,	**come, fill my heart,**	in pain and grief.
		pour out your grace.
Light of all the world,	**enlighten me,**	and give me peace.

1,001 prayers to God the Son

With life like God's,	**I love you, Lord,**	my Saviour, king divine.
You call me friend,		Redeemer of mankind.
	I cling to you,	my Jesus, Word made flesh.
Your friend who failed,		my Jesus, Mary's Son.
Made weak by sins,	**I thank you, Lord,**	my Jesus, full of love.
Confessing guilt,		my Jesus, patient, kind.
	I trust in you,	my Jesus, teaching love.
Forgiven, glad,		you bore your cross for me.
In living faith,	**I mercy seek,**	you died to save mankind.
With joyful hope,		you rose from death to life,
Desiring God,	**I ask for strength,**	my Way, my Truth, my Life.
Accepting pain,		for you are one with God.
In a world of change,	**I live in you,**	my Jesus, God and man.

1,0001 prayers to God the Father

Uniquely made,	**I love you, Lord,**	you made me for yourself.
You give me life,		my Father, mighty God.
Your chosen child,	**I hope in you,**	my Father, wise and good.
With will to choose,		and want to live in you.
	I long for you,	
With mind to know,		eternal God and true.
From depth of soul,	**I seek your help,**	your kingdom come today.
Inclined to sin,		you promise us your life.
With faith in Christ,	**I praise your love,**	your will be done on earth.
Made one with Christ,		for you can do all things.
	I thank you, Lord,	
Restored to life,		you want my heart each day
Created, called,	**I need your care,**	give bread to all your poor.
In time and space,		

1,001 prayers to God the Holy Spirit

Come, Holy Spirit (repeated before each prayer)

third person of God,	**help me,**	to love and serve people in Christ.
with Father and Son,		to teach all that Jesus is Lord.
recalling Christ's word,	**cleanse me,**	to work for Christ's Kingdom today.
supporting our faith,		to live by the teachings of Christ.
affirming our hope,	**move me,**	
our Helper from God,		to live and to die in Christ's Church.
with sevenfold gifts,	**heal me,**	to know and do God's holy will.
explaining God's plan,		to love with my whole heart and soul.
confirming Christ's love,	**guard me,**	to bring Christ's good news to the poor.
to prove sin is bad,		to offer my life to God's work.
remind us of Christ,	**lead me,**	
protecting the Church,		to follow and love Christ my Lord.
abiding with us,	**guide me,**	to show people God's saving love.

Praying from the New Testament

INTRODUCTION

History of the New Testament

When we open a bible today, we see that the first and largest part is called the Old Testament, and the second and more important part is called the New Testament. The Old Testament contains writings describing God's dealing with mankind, and especially with the Jewish people, in the centuries before Christ.

The New Testament starts at the time of Jesus Christ. It consists of 27 writings by various apostles and early teachers of the Church, written at different times, to different people and for different reasons. The writers did not know that what they were writing would later be brought together into a book called the 'New Testament', and considered as part of our bible.

Christ told his apostles to 'go and teach', and they had been teaching for about twenty years before the first letter of the New Testament was written. And the apostles and their followers had been teaching Christ's teaching for over fifty years before the last of the books of the New Testament was written. Then it took many more years before all these writings were copied and spread into the various countries the Church had reached.

At that time, without telephone or radio, without airmail or even steamer mail, letters and messages between different countries were very slow. No wonder it took many years before the 27 writings of the New Testament were all known to Christians of the different countries to which the Church had spread. However most were accepted as holy writings and read to the people by the end of the second century (200 AD). In certain places other works (Gospel of Thomas, Gospel of Peter etc) were found along with them. These were not finally and certainly excluded from the Church's official writings until a decision of the Church leaders at the Council of Hippo in 393, which fixed for us the 27 writings whose writers were inspired by the Holy Spirit.

The book of the Church

The apostles listened to the teaching and guidance of Jesus for the three years of his public life. They continued his work by preaching this Good News to their people. All taught by the spoken word. Only some of them wrote, and they did not write or intend to write the full history or teaching of Jesus. The writers of the Gospels describe the events of less than a hundred days of Jesus' life, each choosing the events and teaching considered useful for his readers.

All the New Testament writings were based on the teachings of the apostles in the early Church. The same Church later assured us that, of all the writings of that time, only the 27 now found in the New Testament were inspired by the Holy Spirit, and are as useful for us as they were for the people they were actually written for. They thus became part of the bible, truly the book of the Church, which we value and read only because of this assurance of the Church.

They remained the book of the Church in later years, when thousands of monks spent their lives copying and recopying the texts by hand, without typewriter or printing. Because of their devoted work, the texts were preserved until the discovery of printing made their reproduction easier and less expensive.

Jesus spoke to his followers in Aramaic, the language of most of his people. Most of the New Testament was written down in Greek, so the writers had to translate the words of Jesus as they wrote. Later these original texts were translated into many other languages, even to the present day. And again, it was from the Church that her members got the assurance that all the translations she approved were accurate versions of the original.

When versions of the bible were produced by other Christian Churches after the Reformation, it was the Church who still guided her people by approving some of these versions, and rejecting others — often because of footnotes which added wrong meanings.

So, it is still to this same Church who wrote, preserved and guaranteed the New Testament, that we turn with confidence today for its explanation and interpretation, because St Peter himself told us that unstable and ignorant people can explain the scriptures falsely, and so bring on their own destruction (2 Peter 3:16).

Praying from the New Testament: Introduction

The New Testament today

Copies of the New Testament are now inexpensive, and most people can read it in their own language. So we are perhaps more than ever today, glad to listen to our Church, as she interprets the writings of her Book for us, and reminds us of its value for each one of us.

The New Testament writers wrote so that their people would believe, trust and love Jesus Christ, and carry out his teaching in their daily lives, in love for him and one another. So as we read their writings today, we too should be led to respond by prayer and holy living, as we wait in joyful hope for our perfect union with Jesus in the life of the Trinity in heaven. We should remember that we are all unique and different persons, with different gifts and talents and vocations, and that each of us must seek help for his or her individual needs in the New Testament, as we apply its lessons to our individual lives.

Listed below are some sample prayer responses suitable for use when we prayerfully read the New Testament, especially when following some of the ways outlined in the following pages.

Lord, I believe and I hope and I love,
help me to please you in all that I do.

O Sacred Heart of Jesus Christ,
be thou my love, my hope, my strength.

Lord, to whom else can we go,
for you have words of lasting life;
and we believe and truly know
that you are Christ the Son of God. (Jn 6:68-69)

I will follow you, Lord, wherever you go.

Lord, in your peace you may send me away
now that I've met Christ my Saviour today. (Luke 2:30)

Lord Jesus Christ, you know all things,
and so you know I love you. (John 21:17)

You are the Christ, the Son of God,
who came to save our sinful world. (Jn 11:27)

Look down in love upon your servant, Lord,
let all be done to me as you have willed. (Luke 1:38)

You are the God of my heart and my life,
my God, whom I've chosen for ever. (Ps 72:6)

Personal prayer

Sometimes the chosen reading will describe actions of Jesus or the apostles and sometimes it will record their teaching. You should first read it carefully — a few times if it is new to you — trying to understand the people being addressed and to identify the people present, and what they said and did. Then you try to picture (or even 'guess') how they felt and reacted, and enter into what is happening by imagining yourself present, perhaps as one of the people or groups you have noticed, and responding *now* in prayer (words, thought and actions): to God the Father who chose and created you in love, and sent Jesus his Son to redeem you; to Jesus Christ now returned to his Father in heaven; or to the Holy Spirit, sent by Father and Son to guide and sanctify the Church and her members today, just as he did in the early Church when the New Testament was being written.

Your prayer from the New Testament is therefore based on your firm faith that the Jesus whose actions and teaching are being described is the very same person who is *now* living with the Father and Holy Spirit in the Trinity of the one God in heaven, loving and caring for us at this moment of time as he loved and cared for the people he lived with in Palestine two thousand years ago. You read about him in the past, but you pray to him NOW.

As you read, therefore, stop after each verse or two, to renew and repeat whatever prayer-responses of love, praise, joy, thanks, petition, etc come to your mind and heart as you relive the scene, action by action.

At times these thoughts and feelings of love etc will be so strong and so clear that you do not need words to express them, and you even find yourself just watching Jesus on the cross or in the stable (for example) with love or joy or sorrow. This is still prayer — just as a mother loves her child by merely holding him and watching him without words.

Praying from the New Testament: Introduction

Praying with others — shared prayer

Every prayer you say, even prayer very personal to you, is a prayer of the Church. You are never alone when praying, because the Church is praying with you, and you with the Church. You never pray merely as an individual, but as a member of the Church, even when there is nobody with you.

Christ has promised 'Where two or three are gathered in my name, I am in their midst'. This leads many to pray *with others*, and you have probably often prayed this way in your family rosary or in a prayer group.

In praying with others from the New Testament, at least one person should personally have prayed the chosen passage beforehand and be prepared to lead the shared prayer. Others should at least know what passage has been chosen, so they too can prepare it if they have time.

The passage is first read slowly and clearly for the group. Then after a pause the leader reads a verse or two and repeats twice a prayer-response chosen as suitable for the needs of the group. All repeat it aloud two or three times, and then spend enough time in silence for each to repeat this or a similar prayer of their own perhaps three or four times.

The shared prayer could end with a suitable hymn, or with a rhythmic prayer-response sung quietly to a familiar tune. Or the group could pray a decade of the rosary, with the Hail Mary addressed to Mary as she lived the event or teaching described in the chosen passage. She was present at many events of the Gospel where she is not mentioned; and in any case she lived the whole New Testament teaching with and in the early Church.

Seven steps for shared meditation

This method was developed at the Lumko Missiological Institute in Africa, and is fully explained with exercises for training prayer leaders, in their booklet 'Starting Neighbourhood Gospel Groups'. It enables group members to be more active and personal in their choice of prayer-response, and to share their experiences with the rest of the group. Its seven basic steps are listed here as a reminder to those who have already used the method:

1 **We invite the Lord** (in prayer)

2 **We read the text**

3 **We look at the text again.**
   — no preaching or discussion!
   — what important words or phrases do we find?
   — we read the text again.

4 **We let God speak to us**
   — silence for 2-5 minutes.

5 **We share what we have heard in our hearts**
   — no preaching or discussion!

6 **We search together**
   — what does the Lord want us to do?
   — how have we lived our WORD OF LIFE?
   — what new WORD will we take home?

7 **We pray together**

Group discussion

This method expands and emphasizes Step Six of the previous method, and will be of greater benefit to group members if each has spent some time in personal prayer beforehand. The leader for the meeting *must* have prepared it beforehand. It loosely follows the 'See, Judge, Act' process devised by Cardinal Cardijn for the Young Christian Workers.

The chosen gospel passage is read section by section; after each section those present try, by pooling their ideas and personal responses:

a *to see* what the author meant to say to the people he was writing for.
b *to judge* whether and how the messages apply to their own lives today, and offer them guidance, example or inspiration.
c *to act* by deciding on some concrete action, personal and/or group.

The first part of the meeting that follows would be devoted to a *review of life*, where members help one another by reporting actions taken as a result of the ACT decision of the previous meeting — but including also any good or bad influences that members feel the world they live in is having on their lives or the lives of others.

Parish renewal scripture sharing

Parish Renewal methods may well help some groups to better sharing. Before the passage is read, a leader should introduce the chosen passage, showing how it fitted into the life of the early Church, and when and where and why it was written. Then after the reading, the leader or somebody else who has prepared it, explains the passage outlining some of its messages for listeners today and suggesting points for prayer. Members are encouraged to take notes during this period of what they find important, in order to use it during the period of silent meditation and prayer that follows.

As part of the meditation and prayer, they are also asked to write an answer to a carefully chosen question, and then to share with the other members of the group from what they have written.

The question may be specially chosen to suit the particular passage of scripture, or it may be a general question that will help all to recognize and express some of the feelings, convictions and prayers that came to them as they listened to, prayed about and meditated on the passage read, e.g.:

'How does the passage encourage or discourage you as a Catholic?'
'How did you react interiorly to the passage — did it upset you, bore you, excite you, gladden you, strengthen you, challenge you? How?'
'What people, teaching, etc, affected you most in this passage? Why?'
'How could it affect your relations with family, neighbours, parish?'

The question is not intended to lead to a discussion of the scripture, or of family and parish needs, but rather to help members of a working group to know, respect and love one another as a result of their sharing, so that they will be more united in their lives of work and prayer.

GUIDE TO SUITABLE
NEW TESTAMENT PASSAGES FOR PRAYER

LIFE OF JESUS FROM THE GOSPELS

Know him more clearly,
love him more dearly,
follow him more nearly

Infancy

Luke 1:26-38   ANNUNCIATION   I am the Lord's servant.
Matt 1:18-25   ST JOSEPH   It is by the Holy Spirit she has conceived.
Luke 1:39-45   VISITATION   Elizabeth was filled with the Holy Spirit.
Luke 1:46-56   MAGNIFICAT   He who is mighty has done great things for me.
Luke 2:1-7   NATIVITY   The time came for her to have her baby.
Luke 2:10-20   THE SHEPHERDS   They saw the baby lying in the manger.
Luke 2:22-24   PRESENTATION   As required by the law of the Lord.
Luke 2:25-35   SIMEON   With my own eyes I have seen your salvation.
Luke 2:36-40   ANNA THE WIDOW   Day and night she worshipped God.
Matt 2:1-12   WISE MEN   They saw the child with Mary and worshipped him.
Matt 2:13-21   ESCAPE TO EGYPT   Take the child and his mother.
Luke 2:41-52   FINDING IN THE TEMPLE   They went back looking for him.
John 2:1-12   CANA WEDDING   His mother said 'Do whatever he tells you.'

Public life: actions and miracles

John 1:1-5, 10-14   INCARNATION   The word became flesh and lived among us.
Matt 3:13-17   BAPTISM OF JESUS   My own dear Son with whom I am pleased.
Matt 4:1-11   JESUS IS TEMPTED   Worship God and serve him alone.
John 1:29-34   THE LAMB OF GOD   He existed before I was born.
John 4:46-53   THE OFFICIAL'S SON   Go, your son will live.
John 5:1-9   THE BETHZADA POOL   Get up, pick up your mat and walk.
Luke 4:38-41   JESUS HEALS   He placed his hands on them and cured them.
Luke 5:12-16   A LEPER IS HEALED   Jesus reached out and touched him.
Luke 5:16-26   PARALYSED MAN   Authority on earth to forgive sins.
Luke 7:1-10   CENTURION   I never found faith like this in Israel.
Luke 7:11-17   WIDOW'S SON'S FUNERAL   His heart was filled with pity.
Mark 4:35-40   STORM AT SEA   Even the wind and waves obey him.
Mark 6:1-6   REJECTED AT NAZARETH   The people did not have faith.
Mark 6:30-44   LOAVES AND FISHES   Everyone ate and had enough.
Matt 14:22-33   WALKING ON THE WATER   Truly you are the Son of God.
Matt 15:21-28   CANAANITE WOMAN   You are a woman of great faith.
Luke 9:28-36   TRANSFIGURATION   This is my Son, listen to him.
John 11:47-54   PHARISEE'S PLOT   Better that one man die for the people.
Luke 17:12-19   GRATITUDE   Ten were healed. Where are the other nine?
Luke 18:25-43   THE BLIND BEGGAR   Jesus, Son of David, have mercy on me.
John 12:1-11   BETHANY MEAL   Why wasn't this money given to the poor.
Mark 11:1-11   PALM SUNDAY   Others spread branches on the road.
Mark 11:15-19   TEMPLE CLEANSING   My temple called a house of prayer.

Public life: teaching and parables

Luke 5:33-39   FASTING EXPLAINED   And then they will fast.
Luke 6:1-11   SABBATH LAW   The Son of Man is the Lord of the Sabbath.
Matt 5:1-12   BEATITUDES   Jesus saw the crowd and began to teach.
Matt 5:13-15   EXAMPLE   Salt for mankind, light for the world.
Matt 5:17-20   GOD'S LAW   Whoever teaches others shall be great.
Matt 5:21-26   ANGER   Go at once and make peace with your brother.
Matt 5:27-32   IMPURITY   Guilty of committing adultery in his heart.
Matt 5:38-42   REVENGE   Do not take revenge, love your enemies.
Matt 6:1-6, 16-18   SHOWING OFF   When you pray do not be like hypocrites.
Matt 6:7-14   THE LORD'S PRAYER   This is how you should pray.
Matt 6:19-23   RICHES   You cannot serve both God and money.
Matt 6:25-34   GOD'S CARE   Seek first God's kingdom and he will provide.
Luke 6:37-42   GENEROSITY   Give to others and God will give to you.
Luke 11:5-13   CONFIDENCE IN PRAYER   Ask and you will receive.
Matt 7:15-20   FALSE PROPHETS   You will know them by what they do.
Matt 7:21-28   OBEY JESUS   Like a wise man who built upon a rock.
Luke 8:19-21, 11:27-28   GOD'S WILL   Hear the word of God and obey it.
Luke 8:4-15   THE SOWER   The seed is the word of God.
Matt 13:24-30, 36-43   THE WEEDS   A man sowed good seeds in his field.
Matt 13:31-33   THE KINGDOM   Like a mustard seed, like a yeast.
Matt 13:44-46   THE KINGDOM   Like a treasure, like a fine pearl.
Matt 18:1-5   HUMILITY   Unless you change and become like children.
Matt 18:6-9   SCANDAL   Cut it off and throw it away.
Luke 15:1-10   LOST SHEEP   I am so happy I have found my lost sheep.
Luke 15:11-32   PRODIGAL SON   This son of mine was dead, now he is alive.
Luke 16:1-13   UNJUST MANAGER   You cannot serve both God and money.
John 10:1-6, 11-18   GOOD SHEPHERD   I know my sheep and they know me.
John 10:22-38   WHY JESUS CAME   I give them eternal life.
Luke 10:25-37   GOOD SAMARITAN   You go then, and do the same.
Luke 12:13-21   A RICH FOOL   Tonight you have to give up your life.
John 10:22-42   JESUS REJECTED   The Father and I are one.
Luke 13:22-30   THE NARROW DOOR   Those who are now last will be first.
Luke 14:7-14   HUMILITY, GENEROSITY   God will repay you.
Luke 14:25-34   DISCIPLESHIP   He gives up everything he has.
Luke 18:1-8   PERSEVERANCE IN PRAYER   She will finally wear me out.
Luke 18:9-14   PHARISEE AND PUBLICAN   God, have pity on me a sinner.
Matt 20:1-16   DAY LABOURERS   Are you jealous because I am generous.
Matt 25:14-30   THREE SERVANTS   Well done, good and faithful servant.
Matt 21:28-32   THE TWO SONS   'Yes sir', he answered, but he did not go.
Luke 14:15-24   THE GREAT FEAST   They all began to make excuses.
Luke 20:27-40   SEVEN HUSBANDS   They will be like angels and cannot die.
Matt 22:34-40   GREATEST COMMANDMENTS   Love God, love your neighbour.
Mark 12:41-44   A WIDOW'S OFFERING   She put more in than all the others.
John 12:20-26   UNSELFISHNESS   He who loves his life will lose it.
John 12:27-36   PROPHECY OF DEATH   I will draw everyone to me.
Matt 25:31-46   FINAL JUDGEMENT   He will divide them into two groups.

Life of Jesus from the Gospels

Public life: saints and sinners

John 1:35-42   FIRST DISCIPLES   Andrew told Peter 'We found the Messiah.'
John 1:43-51   PHILIP, NATHANAEL   We found the one Moses wrote about.
John 2:1-12   WEDDING AT CANA   Mary said, 'Do whatever he tells you.'
John 3:1-21   NICODEMUS   How can a grown man be born again?
John 3:27-36   JOHN TEACHES   Whoever believes in the Son has eternal life.
John 4:5-15   JESUS SPEAKS TO A SAMARITAN   Give me a drink of water.
John 4:16-30   JESUS CONVERTS HER   Come and see the man.
John 4:31-40   THE HARVEST   My food is to obey the one who sent me.
John 5:1-18   JESUS TEACHES   He said God was his own Father.
Matt 4:18-20   CALL OF THE FOUR   I will teach you to catch men.
Luke 4:16-30   JESUS IS REJECTED   The people were filled with anger.
John 1:6-9, 15-18   JOHN THE BAPTIST   God sent his messenger.
Luke 1:5-25   JOHN'S PARENTS   Both lived good lives in God's sight.
Luke 1:67-80   ZECHARIAH PRAYS   Blessed be the Lord God of Israel.
Luke 3:1-6   JOHN'S CALL   The word of God came to John in the desert.
Matt 3:1-6   JOHN PREACHES   Turn away from your sins.
Luke 3:7-14   JOHN INSTRUCTS   Show you have turned away from your sin.
Luke 3:15-18   JOHN TESTIFIES   One is coming who is much greater than I am.
John 1:19-28   JOHN'S MESSAGE   Among you stands one you do not know.
John 1:29-34   JOHN'S WITNESS   The Lamb of God existed before I was born.
John 3:22-27   JOHN'S MISSION   I have been sent ahead of him.
Mark 6:14-29   JOHN'S DEATH   Give me the head of John the Baptist.
Luke 7:18-35   JOHN SENDS DISCIPLES TO ASK   Are you he who is to come?
Luke 7:36-50   MARY THE SINNER   Your faith has saved you. Go in peace.
Luke 8:1-3   DISCIPLES   Women used their own resources to help Jesus.
Luke 5:1-11   FOUR FISHERMEN   They left everything and followed Jesus.
Luke 5:27-32   TAX COLLECTOR   Levi left everything and followed Jesus.
Luke 6:12-16   TWELVE APOSTLES CHOSEN   Jesus went up a hill to pray.
Matt 9:35-38   SHEPHERDS NEEDED   Filled with pity he saw the crowds.
Matt 10:1-11   APOSTLES SENT   Give without being paid.
Matt 10:16, 26-32   APOSTLES ADVISED   Cautious as snakes, gentle as doves.
Matt 10:34-42   APOSTLES SENT   Whoever welcomes you, welcomes me.
John 6:41-51   BREAD OF LIFE   The bread I will give you is my flesh.
John 6:52-59   EUCHARIST PROMISED   He lives in me and I live in him.
John 6:60-70   PETER'S FAITH   You have the words that give eternal life.
Matt 16:21-27   DEATH FORETOLD   These thoughts of yours come from men.
Luke 9:59-62   DISCIPLESHIP   You go and proclaim the kingdom of God.
John 8:1-11   ADULTEROUS WOMAN   I do not condemn you, sin no more.
John 9:1-12   MAN BORN BLIND   I am the light of the world.
John 9:13-34   WITNESS OF CURED MAN   The man knelt down before Jesus.
Luke 10:1-12   72 DISCIPLES   Sent out two by two to go ahead of him.
Luke 10:17-24   DISCIPLES REPORT   Your names are written in heaven.
Luke 10:38-42   MARTHA AND MARY   Mary sat and listened to his teachings.
John 11:1-16   LAZARUS DIES   This happened to bring glory to God.
John 11:17-27   MARTHA'S FAITH   I believe that you are the Son of God.
John 11:28-37   JESUS WEPT   See how much he loved him.
John 11:38-44   RAISING OF LAZARUS   I say this so that they will believe.
Luke 18:15-17   CHILDREN   Let the children come here, do not stop them.
Mark 10:17-31   RICH YOUNG MAN   Sell all you have, and come follow me.
Matt 20:20-38   AMBITION CORRECTED   Be the servant of the rest.
Luke 19:1-10   ZACCHEUS   The Son of man came to seek and save the lost.

Passion and death

Matt 26:31-35 DESERTION PREDICTED This night you will run away.
John 13:31-38 NEW COMMANDMENT Love one another as I have loved you.
John 15:1-10 THE VINE You cannot bear fruit unless you remain in me.
John 15:11-17 CHOSEN FRIENDS You did not choose me, I chose you.
John 15:26-16:15 SPIRIT'S WORK He will lead you into all the truth.
John 16:16-21 SADNESS AND JOY Gladness that no one can take from you.
Matt 26:26-30 EUCHARIST This is my body, This is my blood.
Matt 26:47-56 JESUS CAPTURED The man I kiss is the one you want.
Matt 26:57-68 CAIPHAS AND COUNCIL Tell us if you are the Messiah.
Luke 22:54-62 PETER'S DENIAL Peter went out and wept bitterly.
John 18:28-38 PILATE'S COURT My kingdom does not belong to this world.
Luke 23:6-12 HEROD'S COURT Herod and his soldiers made fun of Jesus.
Luke 23:13-25 INNOCENT CONDEMNED The sentence they were asking for.
Luke 23:13-23 BARABBAS Pilate wanted to set Jesus free.
John 19:1-3 SCOURGING AND CROWNING Pilate had him whipped.
John 19:4-16 DEATH PENALTY Pilate handed Jesus over to be crucified.
Luke 23:26-31 WAY OF THE CROSS The soldiers led Jesus away.
Luke 23:33-49 JESUS FORGIVES They don't know what they are doing.
Mark 15:24-34 JESUS MOCKED My God, my God, why did you abandon me?
John 19:25-30 JESUS DIES Jesus saw his mother standing there.

The risen Christ

Luke 24:1-12 THE WOMEN He is not here, he has been raised.
John 20:1-10 PETER AND JOHN The other disciples went in and believed.
John 20:11-18 MARY MAGDELENE Tell them I am returning to my Father.
Luke 24:13-35 EMMAUS DISCIPLES Stay with us, the day is almost over.
John 20:19-23 THE DISCIPLES He showed them his hands and his side.
John 20:24-29 THOMAS Happy are those who believe without seeing me.
John 21:1-14 DISCIPLES FISHING It is the Lord.
John 21:15-19 PETER Take care of my lambs, take care of my sheep.
John 21:20-25 JOHN The disciple who wrote these things down.
Acts 1:1-10 ASCENSION He was taken up to heaven as they watched.

Life of Jesus from the Gospels

We live in Jesus, he lives in God

Luke 10:21-24   My Father has given me all things.
Luke 23:44-46   Father, in your hands I place my Spirit.
John 5:19-23   What the Father does, the Son also does.
John 8:28-30   He who sent me is with me, I always do what pleases him.
John 14:1-7   There are many rooms in my Father's house.
John 14:8-14   Whoever has seen me has seen the Father.
John 14:18-21   I am in the Father and you are in me.
John 17:1-5   Eternal life means to know God and Jesus Christ.
John 17:6-8   They believe that you sent me.
John 17:9-11   Keep them safe that they may be one as you and I are one.
John 17:20-23   May they be in us, just as you are in me and I am in you.
John 17:24-26   So that the love you have for me may be in them.
Romans 6:1-6   Buried with him in baptism we share his death.
Romans 8:31-39   Who can separate us from the love of Christ.
1 Cor 1:21-31   Christ the Power and Wisdom of God.
1 Cor 10:14-21   When we eat we are sharing the Body of Christ.
1 Cor 11:17-32   You proclaim the Lord's death until he comes.
1 Cor 12:12-14, 25-31   You are Christ's Body and each is a part of it.
1 Cor 13:8-13   When we shall see face to face.
1 Cor 15:42-49   We will wear the likeness of the man from heaven.
2 Cor 1:1-7   Through Christ we share in God's great help.
2 Cor 1:18-22   God makes us sure of our life of union with Christ.
2 Cor 4:1-6   God's glory shining in the face of Christ.
2 Cor 4:6-18   God will take us into his presence.
2 Cor 5:1-10   God will have a house in heaven for us to live in.
2 Cor 5:16-21   God making all mankind his friends through Christ.
Gal 3:26-29   All of you are God's sons in union with Christ Jesus.
Eph 1:1-14   God chose us to be his sons by our union with Christ.
Eph 2:4-13   In our union with Jesus, God raised us up with him.
Phil 2:5-11   The attitude you should have is the one Christ had.
Col 1:15-20   Christ is the visible likeness of the invisible God.
Col 1:24-29   Christ is in you — you will share in the glory of God.
Col 2:6-10   The full content of the divine nature lives in Christ.
Col 3:1-4   Your life is hidden with Christ in God.
1 Tim 2:1-7   Jesus brings God and mankind together.
1 Tim 6:11-16   Win eternal life to which God called you.
2 Tim 2:8-10   God promises eternal life.
Heb 1:1-4   Christ is the exact likeness of God's own being.
Heb 4:12-36   We have a great high priest . . . Jesus the Son of God.
Heb 5:1-10   God declared Jesus to be high priest.
Heb 7:23-28   Jesus lives forever . . . to plead with God for us.
Heb 10:19-31   Jesus opened for us a new way, a living way.
1 Pet 1:1-10   You were chosen according to the purpose of the Father.
2 Pet 1:16-18   We were there when he was given glory by God.
1 John 1:1-4   The word of life existed from the very beginning.
1 John 3:1-3   We shall see him as he really is.
1 John 3:9-10   God's very nature is in him.
1 John 3:19-24   We know that God lives in union with us.
1 John 4:7-15   Whoever loves is a child of God, and knows God.
1 John 4:16-21   We love because God first loved us.
1 John 5:13-15, 20-21   We live with God in union with Jesus Christ.

HOLY SPIRIT SENT BY FATHER AND SON

To make us holy, loving God and neighbour

John 14:15-17, 25-26   The Father will give you another helper.
John 16:5-7, 12-15   The Spirit will lead you into all the truth.
Acts 1:4-9   When the Spirit comes you will be filled with power.
Acts 2:1-13   They were all filled with the Holy Spirit.
Acts 2:14, 36-42   Sins forgiven, you will receive the Holy Spirit.
Eph 1:11-14   God put his ownership on you by giving you the Holy Spirit.
Eph 1:15-23   The Spirit will make you wise and reveal God to you.
Eph 2:14-21   Through Christ all can come in the Spirit to the Father.
Col 1:9-14   Live as the Lord wants and always do what pleases him.
Titus 3:3-7   Who gives us new birth and new life by washing us.
2 Pet 1:19-21   Under control of the Spirit men spoke the message from God.
2 Pet 2:12-15   They lead weak people into the trap.
1 John 2:20-25   The Spirit was poured out on you by Christ.
1 John 2:26-29   His Spirit teaches you about everything.
Romans 5:1-5   God poured out his love into our hearts by the Spirit.
Romans 8:5-11   To be controlled by the Spirit results in life.
Romans 8:12-17   The Spirit makes you God's children.
Romans 8:26-30   The Spirit comes to help us.
1 Cor 2:7-17   To us God made known his secret by means of the Spirit.
1 Cor 3:16-23   You are God's temple and God's Spirit lives in you.
1 Cor 14:1-6   Set your hearts on proclaiming God's message.
1 Cor 12:1-11   The same Spirit gives a different gift to each person.
1 Cor 14:12-17   Make greater use of gifts that build up the Church.
1 Cor 14:18-25   Proclaiming God's message of proof for believers.
1 Cor 14:26-40   Everything must be done in a proper and orderly way.

To explain vices, sins and repentance

Romans 1:28-32   VICE   They are filled with all kinds of wickedness.
Romans 7:14-25   SINFUL NATURE   I don't do the good I want to do.
1 Cor 6:7-11   PUNISHMENT   You have been purified from sin.
1 Cor 6:12-20   IMMORALITY   Use your bodies for God's glory.
1 Cor 9:23-33   SELF-DENIAL   I harden my body and bring it under control.
1 Cor 10:12-13   CONFIDENCE   God will give you strength to endure it.
Gal 5:13-21   VICES   Do not let physical desires control you.
Eph 5:1-5   IMMORALITY   Your life must be controlled by love.
Eph 6:14-20   TEMPTATION   Pray on every occasion as the Spirit leads.
Col 3:5-10   OLD SELF   Put to death earthly desires in you.
2 Thess 3:1-5   PRAYER   God is faithful and will strengthen you.
James 1:2-8   CONFIDENCE   Fortunate when trials come your way.
James 1:12-21   TRIALS   Happy the person who remains faithful.
James 4:1-4   GREED   To be the world's friend means to be God's enemy.
James 5:1-6   RICHES   Weep over the miseries that are coming.
1 Pet 2:11-17   CITIZENSHIP   Live as free people, but as God's slaves.
1 Pet 2:18-25   SUFFERING   Christ left you an example.
1 Pet 4:1-5   PAGAN VICES   They will have to give an account to God.
2 Pet 2:10-15   FALSE TEACHERS   They have left the straight path.
1 John 2:12-17   ENCOURAGEMENT   Do not love the world.

Holy Spirit sent by Father and Son

To explain the duties of daily life

Romans 12:19-21   VIRTUES   Do not let evil defeat you, conquer evil with good.
Romans 13:1-7   GOVERNMENT   Everybody must obey the state authority.
Romans 15:1-7   LOVE OTHERS   Help the weak to carry their burden.
1 Cor 7:1-7   MARRIAGE DUTIES   Each should satisfy the other's needs.
1 Cor 16:1-4   COLLECTION   Each Sunday you must put aside some money.
Eph 5:21-33   MARRIED LOVE   Wives submit ... Husbands love.
Eph 6:1-4   FAMILY LIFE   Duties of children and parents.
Eph 6:5-9   WORK   Work cheerfully ... stop using threats.
Col 3:18-25   FAMILY LOVE   Wives, husbands, children, parents.
1 Thess 4:1-8   MARRIAGE   God did not call us to live in immorality.
1 Thess 5:12-27   LIVE WELL   May God make you holy in every way.
2 Thess 3:6-13   LAZINESS   Whoever refuses to work is not allowed to eat.
1 Tim 6:1-2   WORK ATTITUDES   Slaves and masters.
Heb 12:1-11   PERSEVERANCE   Let us keep our eyes fixed on Jesus.
James 2:14-18   ACTION NEEDED   Faith without action is dead.
1 Pet 1:13-23   REDEEMED   Be holy in all that you do.
James 5:7-11   PATIENCE   We called them happy because they endured.
1 Pet 2:1-3, 9-10   CHOSEN   You are God's own people.
1 Pet 3:8-14   REVENGE   Do not pay back evil for evil.
1 Pet 4:7-11   GENEROSITY   Be self-controlled and alert.
1 Pet 4:12-16. 18   SUFFERING   Full of joy when his glory is revealed.
2 Pet 1:2-11   PROMISED GIFT   To share the divine nature.
1 Pet 5:5-11   HUMILITY   Be alert, be firm in the faith.
1 John 5:1-5   COMMANDMENT   His commands are not too hard for us.
1 John 3:13-18   HATRED   True love shows itself in action.

To help people doing God's work

Eph 3:7-13   PAUL'S CALL   I was made a servant of the Gospel.
Phil 1:3-22   PAUL'S FRIENDS   Helped in the work of the Gospel.
Phil 1:18-26   PAUL'S LOVE   For what is life? For me it is Christ.
Phil 2:19-30   PAUL'S HELPERS   Timothy cares, Epaphroditus worked.
Phil 3:5-14   PAUL'S LOVE   All else thrown away to gain Christ.
Phil 4:1-9   PAUL'S HELPERS   Whose names are in God's book.
Col 1:24-29   PAUL'S WORK   Made a servant of the Church by God.
Col 4:7-13   PAUL'S FELLOW-WORKERS   Tychicus, Onesimus, Mark, etc.
1 Thess 1:2-10   PAUL'S CONVERTS   An example to all believers.
1 Thess 2:1-9   PAUL'S LOVE   Gentle like a mother caring for her children.
1 Thess 2:10-19   PAUL'S CONVERTS   God is at work in you who believe.
1 Tim 1:12-17   PAUL'S SIN   I spoke evil of him and insulted him.
2 Tim 1:2-7   TIMOTHY'S FAITH   The kind his grandmother and mother had.
Romans 1:1-7   PAUL'S ZEAL   I am eager to preach the good news.
Romans 16:8-15   PAUL'S FRIENDS   Phoebe, Priscilla, Aquila, Mary etc.
Romans 16:17-27   PAUL'S FELLOW-WORKERS   Timothy, Lucius, Jason etc.
1 Cor 16:10-19   EARLY CHRISTIANS   Apollos, Stephanas, Achaicus etc.
2 Cor 11:21-33   PAUL'S WORK   Persecutions, travels, dangers etc.
2 Cor 12:1-10   PAUL'S WEAKNESS   When I am weak, then I am strong.

To explain ministry, apostolate and service

Rom 12:3-8   SHARE SERVICE   Though many, we are one body in Christ.
1 Cor 3:4-11   PARTNERS   Each does the work the Lord gave him to do.
Rom 15:14-21   TEACHING   I serve in preaching the Good News.
1 Cor 4:1-17   FAITHFULNESS   Think of us as Christ's servants.
1 Cor 9:16-22   DUTY OF WORK   I become all things to all men.
2 Cor 2:14-36   SENT BY GOD   In union with Christ we are led by God.
2 Cor 4:1-6   COURAGE   God has given us this work to do.
2 Cor 4:6-12   GOD'S WORK   Supreme power belongs to God, not to us.
Gal 1:1-12   FIDELITY   Some are trying to change the Gospel.
Eph 4:7, 11-16   CHURCH WORK   Each has received a special gift.
1 Tim 3:1-13   LEADERS AND HELPERS   Must work and be sincere.
2 Tim 2:1-10   CHURCH WORK   Be strong through the grace that is yours.
2 Tim 4:1-5   TEACHING   I solemnly urge you to preach the message.
Tit 1:5-9   CHURCH   An elder must be without fault.
1 Pet 5:1-4   CHURCH WORK   Work from a real desire to learn.

To explain holiness and virtues

Romans 10:9-17   SALVATION   Faith comes from hearing the message.
Romans 12:1-2   OFFER YOURSELF   As a living sacrifice to God.
Romans 13:8-14   LOVE OTHERS   To love is to obey the whole law.
1 Cor 7:32-35   CELIBACY   Unmarried is trying to please the Lord.
1 Cor 13:1-7   LOVE OTHERS   Love is patient and kind.
2 Cor 4:13-18   CONFIDENCE   We never become discouraged.
2 Cor 8:1-15   ALMSGIVING   Be generous in this service of love.
2 Cor 9:6-15   GENEROSITY   God loves the one who gives gladly.
Gal 6:1-10   LOVE OTHERS   Let us not be tired of doing good.
Eph 4:1-6   UNITY   Live up to the unity God set.
Eph 4:17-24   NEW LIFE   Put on the new self in God's likeness.
Eph 4:25-31   GOOD LIVING   God will set you free.
Eph 5:6-11   LIVE IN LIGHT   Learn what pleases the Lord.
Eph 5:15-21   PRAYER   Find out what the Lord wants you to do.
Eph 5:31-33   MATRIMONY   A sacred truth like Christ and Church.
Phil 2:1-8   UNSELFISHNESS   Look out for one another's interest.
Phil 2:12-18   WITNESS   You must shine among them like stars.
Col 3:1-4   HOLY AIM   Set your heart on the things in heaven.
Col 3:12-17   LOVE PRAYER   God chose you for his own.
Col 4:2-6   PRAYER, INFLUENCE   Give the correct answer to everyone.
1 Thess 4:9-12   WITNESS   Love one another . . . live a quiet life.
1 Tim 6:6-10   FRUGALITY   Food and clothes should be enough for us.
1 Tim 6:17-19   RICHES   Hope not in riches but in God.
Tit 2:1-10   DUTIES OF STATE   Old, young, men, women, slaves.
Heb 13:1-9   MARRIAGE   Keep on loving one another.
Heb 13:15-21   OBEDIENCE   Your leaders watch over your souls.
James 1:9-11   RICHES   Gladness when God sends riches or poverty.
James 1:22-27   ACTION NEEDED   Don't just listen to God's words.
James 2:1-9   HUMAN RESPECT   Never treat people differently.
James 3:1-10   SPEECH   No one has been able to tame the tongue.
James 5:13-19   ADVICE   suffering . . . happy . . . sick . . . sinner.
1 Pet 3:1-7   MARRIED LOVE   Wives submit . . . Husbands respect.
1 Pet 3:15-18   SUFFERING   Explain the hope that is in you.

Holy Spirit sent by Father and Son

To help the Church grow

Acts 1:1-10   ASCENSION   He was taken up to heaven as they watched him.
Acts 1:12-14   WAITING FOR PENTECOST   They gathered to pray as a group.
Acts 2:1-8   PENTECOST   They were all filled with the Holy Spirit.
Acts 2:14-15, 22-24, 32-36   FIRST SERMON   We are all witnesses to this.
Acts 2:38-42   FIRST CONVERTS   Many of them believed the message.
Acts 2:43-47   FIRST BELIEVERS   They shared their belongings.
Acts 3:1-10   FIRST MIRACLES   In the name of Jesus I order you to walk.
Acts 4:1-22   FIRST TRIAL   Which is right — to obey you or to obey God.
Acts 4:23-31   POWER OF PRAYER   Proclaim God's message with boldness.
Acts 4:32-37   UNITY   The believers were one in mind and heart.
Acts 5:17-26   ARREST AND ESCAPE   An angel opened the prison gates.
Acts 5:27-42   GAMALIEL   If it comes from God, you cannot defeat them.
Acts 6:1-7   DEACONS   We will give our full time to prayer and preaching.
Acts 6:8-15, 51-53   FIRST MARTYR   Stephen looked up to heaven.
Acts 8:1-13   SAMARITANS   Philip preached the Messiah to the people.
Acts 8:26-40   ETHIOPIAN   How can I understand unless someone explain.
Acts 9:1-9   CONVERSION OF SAUL   I am Jesus whom you persecute.
Acts 9:10-19   ANANIAS   The Lord sent me so that you might see again.
Acts 9:19-31   SAUL BEGINS WORK   Preaching boldly in the name of Jesus.
Acts 10:34-48   CORNELIUS   God treats everyone on the same basis.
Acts 11:19-30   ANTIOCH   Where believers were first called Christians.
Acts 12:24-13:5   MISSIONARIES   Set apart for me Barnabas and Saul.
Acts 15:1-21   DISPUTE   They met to consider the questions.
Acts 15:22-35   COUNCIL DECISION   The Holy Spirit and we have agreed.
Acts 17:22-34   PAUL AT ATHENS   God is not far from any of you.
Acts 18:1-11   PAUL AT CORINTH   Do not be afraid for I am with you.
Acts 18:24-28   APOLLOS   With great enthusiasm he proclaimed the facts.
Acts 20:17-38   FAREWELL AT EPHESUS   Be shepherds of the Church of God.
Acts 21:3-15   PAUL'S COURAGE   I am ready to die for Jesus.
Acts 22:1-21   PAUL'S VOCATION   I will send you to the Gentiles.
Acts 26:1-11   PAUL'S CONFESSION   I tried to make them deny their faith.
Acts 26:12-18   PAUL'S MISSION   Tell others what you have seen of me.
Acts 26:19-32   PAUL'S ZEAL   That all of you might become what I am.
Acts 28:1-10   PAUL IN MALTA   All other sick people were healed.
Acts 28:16-31   PAUL IN ROME   He welcomed all who came to see him.

To reveal God's plan to John

Rev 2:1-7   EPHESUS   You do not love me as you did at first.
Rev 2:8-11   SMYRNA   I will give you life as your prize.
Rev 2:12-17   PERGAMUM   You did not abandon your faith in me.
Rev 2:18-29   THYATIRA   You are doing more now than you did at first.
Rev 3:1-6   SARDIS   Strengthen what you still have before it dies.
Rev 3:7-13   PHILADELPHIA   They will all know that I love you.
Rev 3:14-22   LAODICEA   I know that you are neither cold nor hot.
Rev 5:6-14   LAMB PRAISED   Praise and honour forever and ever.
Rev 7:9-17   HEAVEN   God will wipe away every tear from their eyes.
Rev 14:1-5   VIRGINS   They follow the Lamb wherever he goes.
Rev 21:1-8   NEW HEAVEN AND EARTH   God's home is with mankind.
Rev 21:22-27   THE HEAVENLY CITY   Nothing that is impure will enter.
Rev 22:6-17   COMING OF JESUS   I will bring my rewards with me.

Praying with God's People

PSALMS OF DAVID

Temptation and suffering (from Psalm 21)
My God, my God, why have you forsaken me?
You are far from my plea and the cry of my distress.
O my God, I call by day and you give no reply;
I call by night and I find no peace.

Yet you, O God, are holy,
enthroned on the praises of Israel.
In you our fathers put their trust;
they trusted and you set them free.
When they cried to you, they escaped.
In you they trusted and never in vain.

But I am a worm and no man,
the butt of men, laughing-stock of the people.
All who see me deride me.
They curl their lips, they toss their heads.
'He trusted in the Lord, let him save him;
let him release him if this is his friend.'

Yes, it was you who took me from the womb,
entrusted me to my mother's breast.
To you I was committed from my birth,
from my mother's womb you have been my God.

Do not leave me alone in my distress;
come close, there is none else to help.
O Lord, do not leave me alone,
my strength, make haste to help me!

Trust in God's guidance (from Psalm 142)

Lord, listen to my prayer:
turn your ear to my appeal.
You are faithful, you are just; give answer.
Do not call your servant to judgment
for no one is just in your sight.

The enemy pursues my soul;
he has crushed my life to the ground;
Therefore my spirit fails;
my heart is numb within me.

I remember the days that are past:
I ponder all your works.
I muse on what your hand has wrought
and to you I stretch out my hands.
Like a parched land my soul thirsts for you.

In the morning let me know your love
for I put my trust in you.
Make me know the way I should walk:
to you I lift up my soul.

Rescue me, Lord, from my enemies;
I have fled to you for refuge.
Teach me to do your will
for you, O Lord, are my God.
Let your good spirit guide me
in ways that are level and smooth.

For your name's sake, Lord, save my life;
in your justice save my soul from distress.
In your love make an end of my foes;
destroy all those who oppress me
for I am your servant, O Lord.

Doing God's will (from Psalm 39)

How many, O Lord my God,
are the wonders and designs
that you have worked for us;
you have no equal.
Should I proclaim and speak of them,
they are more than I can tell!

You do not ask for sacrifice and offerings,
but an open ear.
You do not ask for holocaust and victim.
Instead, here am I.

In the scroll of the book it stands written
that I should do your will.
My God, I delight in your law
in the depth of my heart.

Your justice I have proclaimed
in the great assembly.
My lips I have not sealed;
you know it, O Lord.

I have not hidden your justice in my heart
but declared your faithful help.
I have not hidden your love and your truth
from the great assembly.

O Lord, you will not withhold
your compassion from me.
Your merciful love and your truth
will always guard me.

For I am beset with evils too many to be counted.
My sins have fallen upon me and my sight fails me.
They are more than the hairs of my head
and my heart sinks.

O Lord, come to my rescue,
Lord, come to my aid.
O let there be shame and confusion
on those who seek my life.

For help in old age (from Psalm 70)

In you, O Lord, I take refuge;
let me never be put to shame.
In your justice rescue me, free me:
pay heed to me and save me.

Be a rock where I can take refuge,
a mighty stronghold to save me;
for you are my rock, my stronghold.
Free me from the hand of the wicked,
from the grip of the unjust, of the oppressor.

It is you, O Lord, who are my hope,
my trust, O Lord, since my youth.
On you I have leaned from my birth,
from my mother's womb you have been my help.
Do not reject me now that I am old;
when my strength fails do not forsake me.

But as for me, I will always hope
and praise you more and more.
My lips will tell of your justice
and day by day of your help
though I can never tell it all.

I will declare the Lord's mighty deeds
proclaiming your justice, yours alone.
O God, you have taught me from my youth
and I proclaim your wonders still.

Now that I am old and grey-headed,
do not forsake me, God.
Let me tell of your power to all ages,
praise your strength and justice to the skies,
tell of you who have worked such wonders.
O God, who is like you?

God hears and saves (from Psalm 5)
To my words give ear, O Lord,
give heed to my groaning.
Attend to the sound of my cries,
my King and my God.

It is you whom I invoke, O Lord.
In the morning you hear me;
in the morning I offer you my prayer,
watching and waiting.

But I through the greatness of your love
have access to your house.
I bow down before your holy temple,
filled with awe.

All those you protect shall be glad
and ring out their joy.
You shelter them; in you they rejoice,
those who love your name.

Praise God, our creator (from Psalm 26)
How great is your name, O Lord our God,
through all the earth!

Your majesty is praised above the heavens;
on the lips of children and of babes
you have found praise to foil your enemy,
to silence the foe and the rebel.

When I see the heavens, the work of your hands,
The moon and the stars which you arranged,
what is man that you should keep him in mind,
mortal man that you care for him?

Yet you have made him little less than a god;
with glory and honour you crowned him,
gave him power over the works of your hand,
put all things under his feet.

All of them, sheep and cattle,
yes, even the savage beasts, birds of the air, and fish
that make their way through the waters.

Psalms of David

Loving God (from Psalm 15)
Preserve me, God, I take refuge in you.
I say to the Lord: 'You are my God.
My happiness lies in you alone.'

He has put into my heart a marvellous love
for the faithful ones who dwell in his land.
Those who choose other gods increase their sorrows.
Never will I offer their offerings of blood.

O Lord, it is you who are my portion and cup;
it is you yourself who are my prize.
The lot marked out for me is my delight:
welcome indeed the heritage that falls to me!

I will bless the Lord who gives me counsel,
who even at night directs my heart.
I keep the Lord ever in my sight:
since he is at my right hand, I shall stand firm.

And so my heart rejoices, my soul is glad;
even my body shall rest in safety.
You will show me the path of life,
the fullness of joy in your presence,
at your right hand happiness for ever.

Longing for God (from Psalm 62)
O God, you are my God, for you I long;
for you my soul is thirsting.
My body pines for you
like a dry, weary land without water.
So I gaze on you in the sanctuary
to see your strength and your glory.

For your love is better than life,
my lips will speak your praise.
So I will bless you all my life,
in your name I will lift up my hands.

On you I muse through the night
for you have been my help;
My soul clings to you;
your right hand holds me fast.

For help against enemies (from Psalm 30)

In you, O Lord, I take refuge.
Let me never be put to shame.
In your justice, set me free,
hear me and speedily rescue me.

Be a rock of refuge for me,
a mighty stronghold to save me,
for you are my rock, my stronghold.
For your name's sake, lead me and guide me.

Release me from the snares they have hidden
for you are my refuge, Lord.
Into your hands I commend my spirit.
It is you who will redeem me, Lord.

O God of truth, you detest
those who worship false and empty gods.
As for me, I trust in the Lord:
let me be glad and rejoice in your love.

Have mercy on me, O Lord,
for I am in distress.
Tears have wasted my eyes,
my throat and my heart.

In the face of all my foes
I am a reproach,
an object of scorn to my neighbours
and of fear to my friends.

But as for me, I trust in you, Lord,
I say: 'You are my God.
My life is in your hands, deliver me
from the hands of those who hate me.'

How great is the goodness, Lord,
that you keep for those who fear you,
that you show to those who trust you
in the sight of men.

Save me from my sinfulness   (from Psalm 68)

Save me, O God,
for the waters have risen to my neck.

I am wearied with all my crying,
my throat is parched.
My eyes are wasted away
from looking for my God.

How can I restore
what I have never stolen?
O God, you know my sinful folly;
my sins you can see.

Let those who hope in you not be put to shame
through me, Lord of hosts:
let not those who seek you be dismayed
through me, God of Israel.

It is for you that I suffer taunts,
that shame covers my face,
that I have become a stranger to my brothers,
an alien to my own mother's sons.
I burn with zeal for your house
and taunts against you fall on me.

This is my prayer to you,
my prayer for your favour.
In your great love, answer me, O God,
with your help that never fails:
rescue me from sinking in the mud;
save me from my foes.

Lord, answer, for your love is kind:
in your compassion, turn towards me.
Do not hide your face from your servant;
answer quickly for I am in distress.
Come close to my soul and redeem me;
ransom me pressed by my foes....
As for me in my poverty and pain
let your help, O God, lift me up.

God's knowledge and Law (from Psalm 138)

O Lord, you search me and you know me,
you know my resting and my rising,
you discern my purpose from afar.
You mark when I walk or lie down,
all my ways lie open to you.

Before ever a word is on my tongue
you know it, O Lord, through and through.
O where can I go from your spirit,
or where can I flee from your face?
If I climb the heavens, you are there.
If I lie in the grave, you are there.

If I take the wings of the dawn
and dwell at the sea's furthest end,
even there your hand would lead me,
your right hand would hold me fast.

For it was you who created my being,
knit me together in my mother's womb.
I thank you for the wonder of my being,
for the wonders of all your creation.

Already you knew my soul,
my body held no secret from you
when I was being fashioned in secret
and moulded in the depths of the earth.

Your eyes saw all my actions,
they were all of them written in your book;
every one of my days was decreed
before one of them came into being.

To me, how mysterious your thoughts,
the sum of them not to be numbered!
If I count them, they are more than the sand;
to finish, I must be eternal, like you.

O search me, God, and know my heart.
O test me and know my thoughts.
See that I follow not the wrong path
and lead me in the path of life eternal.

Psalms of David

Praise of God's mercy (from Psalm 85)

Turn your ear, O Lord, and give answer
for I am poor and needy.
Preserve my life, for I am faithful:
save the servant who trusts in you.

You are my God, have mercy on me, Lord,
for I cry to you all the day long.
Give joy to your servant, O Lord,
for to you I lift up my soul.

O Lord, you are good and forgiving,
full of love to all who call.
Give heed, O Lord, to my prayer
and attend to the sound of my voice.

Among the gods there is none like you, O Lord;
nor work to compare with yours.
All the nations shall come to adore you
and glorify your name, O Lord:
for you are great and do marvellous deeds,
you who alone are God.

I will praise you, Lord my God, with all my heart
and glorify your name for ever;
for your love to me has been great:
you have saved me from the depths of the grave.

The proud have risen against me;
ruthless men seek my life:
But you, God of mercy and compassion,
slow to anger, O Lord,
abounding in love and truth,
turn and take pity on me.

O give your strength to your servant
and save your handmaid's son.
Show me a sign of your favour
that my foes may see to their shame
that you console me and give me your help.

Loving and praising God   (from Psalm 41)

Like the deer that yearns for running streams,
so my soul is yearning for you, my God.

My soul is thirsting for God, the God of my life;
when can I enter and see the face of God?

These things will I remember
as I pour out my soul:
how I would lead the rejoicing crowd
into the house of God,
amid cries of gladness and thanksgiving,
the throng wild with joy.

Why are you cast down, my soul,
why groan within me?
Hope in God; I will praise him still,
my saviour and my God.

Mercy and praise   (from Psalm 56)

Have mercy on me, God, have mercy
for in you my soul has taken refuge.
In the shadow of your wings I take refuge
till the storms of destruction pass by.

I call to God the Most High,
to God who has always been my help.
May he send from heaven and save me
May God send his truth and his love.

O God, arise above the heavens;
may your glory shine on earth!
My heart is ready, O God, my heart is ready.
I will sing, I will sing your praise.

I will thank you, Lord, among the peoples,
among the nations I will praise you
for your love reaches to the heavens
and your truth to the skies.

O God, arise above the heavens;
may your glory shine on earth!

God's Law — my joy (Psalm 118, 2)

How shall the young remain sinless?
By obeying your word.
I have sought you with all my heart:
let me not stray from your commands.
I treasure your promise in my heart
lest I sin against you.
Blessed are you, O Lord;
teach me your statutes.
With my tongue I have recounted
the decrees of your lips.
I rejoiced to do your will
as though all riches were mine.
I will ponder all your precepts
and consider your paths.
I take delight in your statutes;
I will not forget your word.

God's Law — my delight (Psalm 118, 3)

Bless your servant and I shall live
and obey your word.
Open my eyes that I may see
the wonders of your law.
I am a pilgrim on the earth;
show me your commands.
My soul is ever consumed
as I long for your decrees.
You threaten the proud, the accursed,
who turn from your commands.
Relieve me from scorn and contempt
for I do your will.
Though princes sit plotting against me
I ponder on your statutes.
Your will is my delight;
your statutes are my counsellors.

God's Law teaches me (Psalm 118, 9)

Lord, you have been good to your servant
according to your word.
Teach me discernment and knowledge
for I trust in your commands.
Before I was afflicted I strayed
but now I keep your word.
You are good and your deeds are good;
teach me your statutes.
Though proud men smear me with lies
yet I keep your precepts.
Their minds are closed to good
but your law is my delight.
It was good for me to be afflicted,
to learn your statutes.
The law from your mouth means more to me
than silver and gold.

God's Law — my maker's instructions (Psalm 118, 10)

It was your hands that made me and shaped me:
help me to learn your commands.
Your faithful will see me and rejoice
for I trust in your word.
Lord, I know that your decrees are right,
that you afflicted me justly.
Let your love be ready to console me
by your promise to your servant.
Let your love come and I shall live
for your law is my delight.
Shame the proud who harm me with lies
while I ponder your precepts.
Let your faithful turn to me,
those who know your will.
Let my heart be blameless in your statutes
lest I be ashamed.

God's Law — my wisdom   (Psalm 118, 13)

Lord, how I love your law!
It is ever in my mind.
Your command makes me wiser than my foes;
for it is mine for ever.
I have more insight than all who teach me
for I ponder your will.
I have more understanding than the old
for I keep your precepts.
I turn my feet from evil paths
to obey your word.
I have not turned from your decrees;
you yourself have taught me.
Your promise is sweeter to my taste
than honey in the mouth.
I gain understanding from your precepts
and so I hate false ways.

God's Law — my light   (Psalm 118, 14)

Your word is a lamp for my steps
and a light for my path.
I have sworn and have made up my mind
to obey your decrees.
Lord, I am deeply afflicted:
by your word give me life.
Accept, Lord, the homage of my lips
and teach me your decrees.
Though I carry my life in my hands,
I remember your law.
Though the wicked try to ensnare me
I do not stray from your precepts.
Your will is my heritage for ever,
the joy of my heart.
I set myself to carry out your statutes
in fullness, for ever.

God's Law shows his love (Psalm 118, 19)

I call with all my heart; Lord, hear me,
I will keep your statutes.
I call upon you, save me
and I will do your will.
I rise before dawn and cry for help,
I hope in your word.
My eyes watch through the night
to ponder your promise.
In your love hear my voice, O Lord;
give me life by your decrees.
Those who harm me unjustly draw near:
they are far from your law.
But you, O Lord, are close:
your commands are truth.
Long have I known that your will
is established for ever.

God's Law protects me (Psalm 118, 20)

See my affliction and save me
for I remember your law.
Uphold my cause and defend me;
by your promise, give me life.
Salvation is far from the wicked
who are heedless of your statutes.
Numberless, Lord, are your mercies;
with your decrees give me life.
Though my foes and oppressors are countless
I have not swerved from your will.
I look at the faithless with disgust;
they ignore your promise.
See how I love your precepts;
in your mercy give me life.
Your word is founded on truth:
your decrees are eternal.

God's Law — my treasure (Psalm 118, 21)

Though princes oppress me without cause
I stand in awe of your word.
I take delight in your promise
like one who finds a treasure.
Lies I hate and detest
but your law is my love.
Seven times a day I praise you
for your just decrees.
The lovers of your law have great peace;
they never stumble.
I await your saving help, O Lord,
I fulfil your commands.
My soul obeys your will
and loves it dearly.
I obey your precepts and your will;
all that I do is before you.

God's Law — my support (Psalm 118, 22)

Lord, let my cry come before you:
teach me by your word.
Let my pleading come before you;
save me by your promise.
Let my lips proclaim your praise
because you teach me your statutes.
Let my tongue sing your promise
for your commands are just.
Let your hand be ready to help me,
since I have chosen your precepts.
Lord, I long for your saving help
and your law is my delight.
Give life to my soul that I may praise you.
Let your decrees give me help.
I am lost like a sheep; seek your servant
for I remember your commands.

PEOPLE OF THE GOSPEL

Jesus Christ, his Mother and his friends

Zachary's prayer (Luke 1:68-79, adapted)
O blessed God of Israel, Lord,
you promised long ago,
to visit us and set us free
from sin that slaves our will.

Fulfilling now your promises,
you send us Jesus Christ,
to save us from our enemies,
and all that harms our lives.

So, saved from sin and free from fear,
we now can love and serve,
in holiness and goodness, Lord,
each day that we will live.

O God most high, help me, your child,
to be your prophet here,
to go before you to your friends,
preparing hearts for you.

To tell them you are merciful,
and tender in your love.
To tell them they can too be saved,
when you forgive their sins.

For each day you send your Son,
to light our darkened minds,
to take away blind fear of death,
and guide us in your peace. (Possible tune: Amazing Grace)

The Angelus (adapted)

The angel came, O Mary, to announce
that God had chosen you to bear his Son.
With love you answered, 'I'm your servant, Lord.
Let all be done to me as you have planned'.
> *Hail Mary, full of grace, God now lives with you.*
> *Blessed of women, praised be Christ your Son.*
> *Hail, holy Mary, Mother of our God.*
> *pray for us sinners, now and as we die.*

The Word then taking flesh within your womb,
came down to us to live as God and man.
We pray, most holy Mother of our God,
that all Christ promised us will be fulfilled. *Hail* . . .

Pour out, O Lord, your grace on us who learned,
by angel's message, that your Son took flesh.
And grant us by his passion and his death,
to share the glory of his risen life. *Hail* . . .

(Possible tune: Soul of my Saviour)

Mary's prayer (Magnificat, Luke 1:45-55, adapted)

Father, my spirit loves and adores you,
finding in you all joy and delight.
Though I am nothing, bless'd will my name be,
servant of yours, Lord, safe in your love.

Show us your power, humbling the mighty,
checking the strong and raising the low.
Helping the weak ones, feeding the poor ones,
sending the wealthy empty away.

Wondrous your actions, planned for my joy, Lord,
Almighty Father, holy your name.
Ages to ages, love and compassion,
pour out upon us, fearing your name.

Guarding your people, never refusing
your loving mercy, endlessly ours.
Mercy you promised, promised our race, Lord,
Abraham's children, people of yours.

(Possible tune: Bunessan — Morning has broken)

Petitions from the Lord's Prayer

God, almighty Father, through eternal love,
you made us your children; heaven's our true home.
We live but a few years in this changing world,
brothers all and sisters, chosen to be friends.

May your name be holy, known and loved and praised,
by your people living in the world you gave.
Your true life is hidden from our human minds,
but our lips and voices praise your holy name.

May you be our King, Lord, whom we all obey,
offering our service, though we often fail.
While we wait in exile, living in your love,
as our King we choose you, may your Kingdom come.

May all people freely know and love your plan,
doing your will always, keeping your commands,
loving you with whole heart, joyful, happy, glad,
as the saints and angels do in heav'n above.

Seeking what we need, Lord, first we ask for bread,
bread the poor need daily, just that they may live.
And when all have bread, Lord, then we ask for more:
for all other needs, of body and of soul.

Lord, because you love us, pardon us our sins,
as we pardon others sinning against us.
In our bitter feelings, we recall Christ's love,
who forgave the people who brought him to his death.

Lord, preserve us always, in our trials and tests;
do not let us suffer more than we can bear.
Hold us in your hand, Lord, give us help and strength,
to resist temptation, steadfast against sin.

Save us and our friends, Lord, all our fellow-men,
from all pain and sorrow, caused by human sin.
But as our sins added to the world's pain,
help us bear our fair share, measured by your love.

(Possible tune: Jesus, thou art coming)

RESPONDING TO JESUS'S LAST SUPPER TALK

Love and desire   (based on John 13:31-38)

Lord Jesus Christ, in your passion and death,
you showed us the glory and power of your love,
and so revealed to us the glory and power of God
   who is love.

And as God's glory was shown to us, Lord Jesus,
through the love of your human life and death,
I believe that when we die you will show to us
the glory of your divine life in heaven,
one with the Father and Holy Spirit for evermore.

Lord Jesus, you have left this world
and gone back to the Father in heaven.
We look for you, we seek you, we long for you.
But we cannot yet join you in your new life,
because you want us to show those with whom we live
   your new commandment,
that we should love one another as you have loved us.

Help us to love one another so well, Lord Jesus,
that everyone will know that we are your followers,
whom you have sent to teach others your love.

Jesus, I desire to know where you have gone.
I know I cannot follow you now,
but I hope that I will follow you later,
when my work in this world is completed.

Lord Jesus, I long so much for you,
and want so much to be with you,
that like Peter, I am willing to die now for you.
But my time has not yet come,
and I am not yet ready to be with you in heaven.
Keep me from sin, Lord Jesus,
while I finish the life you want me to live here.
Keep your hand on me today, and every day,
lest I betray you and deny you through sin.   Amen.

Knowing the Father (based on John 14:1-14)

Lord Jesus, I believe in you and in God your Father.
I will not be afraid or troubled in heart,
for I know you have gone to prepare a place for me,
a place in your Father's house, Lord Jesus,
where there is room for everyone,
a special place for each person you love.
I believe you will return and take me to yourself
so that I will be for ever where you are.

Jesus, I know this only because I believe your word.
I cannot directly know 'heaven' where you now live;
my human mind cannot even understand it.
But I know how to get there, for you are the *way*,
and you are the *truth* and you are the *life*.

The apostles met you daily in your human life, Lord,
and through you learned to know the Father
who is with you and in you.
When I meet you today in prayers of faith and love,
I can also know the Father who is with you in heaven,
living in you while you live in him.

For everything you did on earth, Lord Jesus,
including all the apostles saw and heard,
was done by the Father, united to you as God,
living in you as you lived in him.
The apostles believed for they saw your miracles,
miracles that could not be done by a man alone,
but which showed the power of God working in you.
And because I also believe you, Lord Jesus Christ,
I know I can do the same and even greater works,
if I allow your Father to work through me and in me,
for in leaving this world in your human life
you left me and all your people here in your place.
Help me to carry on your work and to seek your glory,
and you will grant whatever I ask in your name,
so that the Father's glory that is shown through you,
may also be shown to others through me.

Responding to Jesus' Last Supper talk

Truth and peace (based on John 14:15-31)

Lord Jesus Christ, I love you,
and I promise and intend to keep your commandments,
but I know I need your help.
You promised to send your Spirit to the apostles,
to help them in the work you entrusted to them.
I know your Spirit through my faith in your word.
He is the Spirit who reveals the truth about God.
He is the Helper who will remain with us forever.
I thank you, Lord Jesus, for the help of your Spirit,
whom the Father sends to your Church in your name,
to teach us everything we need to know,
and to help us remember all you have taught us.
So, even though you have ascended to heaven,
I am not alone, for your Spirit is with me,
and he remains with me and in me,
and speaks to me through your Church today,
as he spoke through the apostles you sent.

Lord, I look forward to seeing you face to face,
I hope to know you as you really are,
and to know just how you are in the Father,
and how I am in you, and how you are in me.
Jesus, I love you. I want to obey your teaching.
I am glad that your Father loves me,
and guides me with his law,
and comes with you to live in me.

Lord Jesus Christ, my human heart longs for peace.
Give me your peace, a peace the world cannot give.
In your peace, and confident of your love,
I will not be worried or upset.
I am glad that you have returned to your Father
taking our human nature with you into the Trinity
into union with your Father and Holy Spirit.
For the presence of your body and soul in heaven
is a pledge and sign of the heavenly destiny
of the bodies and souls of your human friends,
all the people you created and love.

Union with Jesus (based on John 15:1-10)

Jesus, you have called me to be united to you,
as a branch is united to a vine.

United to you, I can be cleansed and made holy,
by the trials and difficulties of this life.
United to you, I share in your life,
and you work with me and through me,
and I will bear much fruit.
United to you, I can ask for anything I want,
and I will have it.
United to you, I will follow your teaching,
and become your disciple and friend.

Lord Jesus, I can do nothing without you.
Separated from you by sin,
I become like a dead branch,
unable to love you,
unable to bear fruit for you,
unable to do the work you choose me for,
good only to be thrown out and burned.

Lord Jesus, save me from my weakness.
Protect me, and help me, and keep me from sin,
so that I may live in you and work for you always.

I am confident, Lord Jesus Christ,
because I know you love me with a divine love,
just as your Father loves you.
I want to remain in your love and enjoy your love.
To remain in your love, I obey your commands,
as you obeyed your Father's command,
and remain in his love.

Responding to Jesus' Last Supper talk

Glad to obey Jesus (based on John 15:11-17)

Lord Jesus Christ, I thank you for loving me,
for working and suffering, to make me happy,
for you desire to fill me with your joy.
For my happiness you made known your command:
'Love one another as I have loved you.'
And you loved me with the greatest love possible,
for you gave your life for me.

Lord Jesus, I want to love you, and be your friend.
To please you, I will keep your commandments,
for you gave me your commandments for my welfare,
showing me the best way to live.
Because you are my friend, you taught me your law.
Because I am your friend, I will obey you in love.
And being your friend, and not just a paid servant,
I know and rejoice in your love, Lord Jesus.
I know your mind, and I know your plan.
When you called me to be your friend,
you opened to me the mind and love of your Father,
by showing me that the Father loves me,
and gives me his law as my 'Maker's Instructions'.
I did not choose you as my friend, Lord Jesus,
— for I have neither right or power to do so —
but you chose me to be your friend,
and sent me into your world, to your people,
so that my life would bear the fruit you want,
fruit that will last for ever,
and that I will fully know only in heaven.

I trust, Lord Jesus, in your Father's love.
You and the Father are united in heaven,
and together you live with me in my daily life,
and he will give me whatever I can ask in your name.
Help us all to obey your law and love one another,
to work for one another's happiness and welfare,
and to make this world a better place for all.

Sent to the world (based on John 15:18-27)

As I kneel before you in love, Lord Jesus,
I remember that the sinful world hated you
when you came to pour out your love upon us.
If I belonged to the world, following sinful people,
the world would love me as its own.
But you have chosen me out of the world,
to be your follower and your special friend,
and so the world despises me and hates me.
As your friend, I am ready to share your life,
and because I am yours, called to be your friend,
some will persecute me, and some will listen to me,
as some persecuted you, and some obeyed you.
Like you, I can be a sign that many will reject,
showing their hidden thoughts and sinfulness,
rejecting the teaching they hear through me,
and so rejecting your love, and your Father's love.

In his gift of freedom to mankind, Lord Jesus,
your Father knew that some would freely disobey.
But you did not let this affect your teaching;
you did not leave people in ignorance,
for you knew that the love of those who obey
is more important than the sin of those who disobey,
and the happiness that comes from following your way,
is more valuable than the suffering that follows sin,
and, with your gift of freedom, we must accept both.

You prayed for those who sinned, to be converted,
and commended them to the mercy of your Father.
And in accepting your sufferings and death,
you accepted and ended the result of their sin.

So, because of the love you have shown me,
I must continue to speak about you, Lord Jesus,
and to explain your message to all who listen,
because your Holy Spirit, our Helper, has come
to help me understand your teaching,
and to give me strength to speak about you.

Responding to Jesus' Last Supper talk

Guided by the Spirit (based on John 16:1-15)

I turn to you, Lord Jesus, in faith and love.
You teach me to continue to believe in you
when I am rejected or persecuted,
by people who do not know you or your Father,
and who may think they are 'serving God'
when they oppose me, or even try to kill me.

You told the apostles these things, Lord Jesus,
for you knew they would be sad when you left them.
Lord, I am not sad that I cannot see or hear you,
for this is your plan for me and my time,
and you have sent the Holy Spirit to guide me,
to reveal the truth about God to human minds,
to lead me and all God's people into full truth,
not by making a new revelation,
but by helping us understand what you taught us.

Your Spirit, Lord, led many people to you
through the preaching of the apostles.
By showing their sinfulness in not believing in you,
he proved that they and their leaders were wrong
in thinking you guilty of sin.
He proved they were unjust in condemning you,
by showing that you are now risen to the Father.
He proved they were wrong in their judgement,
for in your death, *they* did not overcome *you*,
but you overcame the power of evil and sin.

Lord Jesus, I believe in your Holy Spirit
living in you and guiding your Church today,
living in me and in all your people,
helping us to see and reject the lies of the world
that you overcame by your death,
and helping us to turn to your apostles and to your Church
to learn the right way to live.

Spreading the Good News (based on John 17:1-13)

Father in heaven, give me your life and power,
so that I may glorify you in my work.
You chose me for life, and sent me into your world,
so that I might continue the work of your Son,
who brought eternal life to all those you gave him,
the eternal life of knowing you, the one true God,
and of knowing him, Jesus Christ whom you sent,
who finished his work on earth
and is now glorified with you in heaven
with the glory he had before the world was made.

Lord, help me to continue his work today
for this is why you chose me and sent me.
Help me to make you known to your people,
to my friends, my neighbours, my fellow-workers.
Help me to make the world a better place to live in,
by changing whatever leads to sin and suffering,
and by supporting whatever helps us to a better life.

Help me to live and to teach only your message,
the message you gave Jesus and he gave the apostles,
so that all may know our message is from you.
Help them to believe and to know
that you sent your Son, Jesus Christ,
to the people of his country and time,
that Jesus sent his Church
to people of all countries till the end of time,
and that his Church now sends me to my world,
and especially to those I meet here today.

O Lord God, my Father,
listen to the prayer of your Son for his people,
the prayer I repeat in and for his Church today;
'Lord, keep us safe by the power of your name,
so that we may be one, as Jesus is one with you.'

Responding to Jesus' Last Supper talk

Working for God (based on John 17:14-20)

O God my Father, I believe the message of your Son,
about your love and the sinfulness of the world,
and his warning that the world would hate me,
if I refused to belong to the world,
as it hated him before me,
when he refused to belong to the world.

Lord, I do not ask to be taken out of the world,
because Jesus sent me here as you sent him.
But keep me safe from sin and from the evil one.
Make me holy and good, as Jesus your Son was.
I offer myself completely to you,
to live fully the truth you sent me through Jesus.

Help all of us who believe your message
to pass it on to others
by our influence and good example.
Help us to be united to one another in love.
As Jesus lives in you, and you live in Jesus,
help us to live in Jesus,
so that we also live in you, and you live in us.
You live in Jesus and Jesus lives in us;
unite us therefore to one another in this world,
so that all can see that you have sent us,
and that you love us as you love Jesus.

Father, you have given us to Jesus your Son,
to be his followers and his friends,
and he wants us to remain always with him,
and to see and share his life after we die,
in the glory he enjoyed before the world was made.
O God my Father, the world does not know you,
but Jesus knows you, and we know that you sent him
to make you known while he was on earth.
We are glad that he continues to make you known
through the Spirit of Love whom you send us;
through the Spirit's power and love he stays with us
as we live and work for you in our world today.

RESPONDING TO EPISTLES

The love of Christ (from Romans 8)

Heavenly Father, your Holy Spirit comes to help us,
because we are weak.
We do not even know how to pray,
so the Spirit himself pleads with you for us,
in groans that words cannot express.
And you, who see into the hearts of men,
know the thoughts and desires
the Spirit puts into our hearts;
for the Spirit pleads with you on our behalf,
in accordance with your will.

If you are with us, O God,
who can be against us?
You did not keep your own Son to yourself
but offered him for us all.
You gave us your Son:
will you not freely give us everything we need?
Christ Jesus, who died for us,
who was raised to life,
and who is now sitting at your right hand,
is pleading with you for us.

Who then can separate us from the love of Christ?
Can trouble do it, or hardship, or persecution,
or hunger, or poverty, or danger, or death?
No, in all these things, we have complete victory
through Jesus Christ who loves us.
For I am certain, Father,
that nothing can separate us from his love,
which he pours out on us from you —
neither death nor life,
neither angels nor other heavenly rulers or powers;
neither the present nor the future;
neither the world above nor the world below.
There is nothing in all creation
that will ever be able to separate us from your love
that is ours through Jesus Christ, our Lord.

Responding to Epistles

Doing God's will (from Romans 11 and 12)

How deep is your knowledge, Lord!
How rich your wisdom!
How impossible for anyone to grasp your plan,
or understand the reasons for your actions!
Who could ever know your mind
or presume to advise you?
Who could give you anything that is not already yours?
All things come from you, and exist through you,
to whom be glory for ever.

I remember your mercy, Lord.
As a child made to your likeness, I worship you.
I give you my living body as a holy sacrifice,
offering all my powers that I may know and love you.
Help me not to imitate the sinful ways of the world,
but let me change my whole way of life,
through the new mind I receive from Jesus Christ.
Thus I will know myself that your will is for my good,
and what you want is the most perfect thing I can do.

Help me not exaggerate my real importance,
but to look on myself with the eyes of faith:
knowing that I am loved, respected and chosen by you,
and that everything I have has been given me by you;
knowing that I am united to all Christians in Christ,
as different parts of the body are united in one body.
My vocation in the Church is uniquely mine alone.
No one else can give the love and service that I can.
I am not judged by the type of work I do,
but by the way I do it according to your gifts,
teaching and guiding others because of my faith,
serving others in unselfishness,
gladly giving time and money for others.
Help me to respect and love others
because they also are loved by you,
and chosen to fulfil their part in your infinite plan.

Strengthen me in my work. Sustain me in my trials.
Help me to keep on praying all through my life.

Serving Jesus Christ (Romans 12)

Almighty Father of my Lord Jesus Christ,
I offer myself to you, as a living sacrifice,
devoted to your service and pleasing to you.
Help me to reject the false standards of this world.
Turn my mind to you inwardly and completely,
to know what is good and perfect and pleasing to you.

Lord, keep me from pride and vanity
so that I can offer you the work you want from me.
Let me not think of myself more highly than I should.
Help me to see myself as I really am,
to know myself as you know me:
as someone loved by you in spite of many failures,
as someone forgiven by you in spite of many sins.

Father I rejoice in my union with Jesus Christ,
You have made me different from all others you created,
but you have called me to be one with them in Jesus.
Made into one body in union with him
and united as different parts of the same body,
we can all use our different gifts for you
in accordance with the grace you have given us.

Help me, Lord, to use for your work
the special gifts you have given to me.
Give me the faith to speak your message to all.
Help me to serve those who are in need,
to teach those who are ignorant,
to encourage those who are weak and downhearted,
to be cheerful in my kindness to others,
to use my authority over others for their welfare,
and to accept the guidance and authority of others.

Help me, Father, as one united to Jesus your Son,
to be like him in my sincere love,
and to work hard without laziness.
Give me his mind to love good and hate evil.
Give me his love to serve you and to respect others,
always joyful in my hope, patient in my troubles,
and always glad to accept the work entrusted to me.

Responding to Epistles

Working for Jesus (1 Corinthians 3:4-11)

I am your servant, Lord Jesus Christ,
because you called me, and led me to believe,
and showed me the work you wanted me to do.

With all your servants and friends in the Church,
I am called to spread your Good News and love today.
Sometimes I plant the seed,
and sometimes I water the young plant,
but it is your Father in heaven
who gives life to the plant and makes it grow;
and so, the Word planted and tended by human effort,
will bear abundant fruit in the lives of those we serve,
and God will reward us for what we do.
Help me and all my fellow-workers
to remain united with you,
working together, as partners in your Father's field,
among the people to whom he sends us.

Let our work be founded on you, Lord Jesus Christ,
like a house built on strong foundations.
Help us to pray and work so that those we serve
may become temples of God, your Father,
with your Holy Spirit living in them.
Help us not to be jealous of others who work for you.
Help us not to quarrel with one another,
or to seek after the wisdom of this world
which is nonsense in the sight of your Father.

Help us never to boast about our success,
for when we work for you, Lord Jesus,
everything belongs to us:
everything in this world and the next,
everything in life and in death,
in the present and in the future —
all belong to us, not because of our own efforts
but because we belong to you, Lord Jesus,
and you belong to God,
united with him in the unity of the Spirit
for ever and ever.

God's loving plan (Ephesians 1)

We thank you, God, Father of our Lord Jesus Christ,
for you have blessed us in him with spiritual gifts.
Before the world was made
you had already chosen us for life,
chosen us to be yours,
chosen us to be yours in Christ,
and to be holy and sinless before you.
And in choosing us you had already decided
that through Christ you would make us your children.
We thank you for this plan which pleased your love,
and we praise you for your love in carrying it out,
through the free gift you gave us in your dear Son.

For by the death of Christ,
we are set free and our sins are forgiven.
How great is your love, O Lord and Father,
which you gave us in such abundance!
In your divine understanding and wisdom
not merely do you carry out your plan,
but you make it known to us your people —
the hidden plan that you will complete through Jesus,
to bring all creation together, with Christ as head,
everything you made in heaven and on earth,
because you loved it.

All things are done according to your plan,
You chose us in union with Christ to be your people,
through the free choice and purpose of your love,
as you had decided from the beginning of creation.
We have heard your message of truth,
the good news that brings us salvation.
We believe in Christ, and you seal us as your own,
by giving us the Holy Spirit you promised us.
The Spirit is the guarantee that we will receive
the further gifts you have promised your people,
when you will give us whom you have chosen
full freedom and help to love and serve you
every day of our life.

Responding to Epistles

Praising God's love (from Ephesians 3)

We kneel before you, Father.
From the riches of your glory and love,
strengthen the hidden life of our souls
through your Spirit and his grace.
May Christ live in our hearts through faith.
May our lives be rooted and founded in love.
May we, like all the holy people who love you,
be able to experience your love to the full,
in its breadth, its length, its height and its knowledge.

May we understand and live by your mystery,
which you now make known through your apostles,
that all men are called in Jesus Christ,
to win the same inheritance,
to be part of the same body,
and to share in the same divine promise.

By the gift of your grace, which makes me powerful,
help me, the least of your people,
to spread to all people the good news of Christ's love,
even though my human mind can never fully grasp it.
Help me to make known to all people your loving plan,
hidden by you from the beginning of time,
and now made known through your eternal plan
in your whole Church, by Christ Jesus our Lord.

Help me to live my life with joy,
strengthened through my faith in you,
that the example of my life, even in suffering,
may help others by showing them your love.
In the Church and in Christ Jesus for ever,
may all glory be to you, O good God,
whose power is working in us through love,
to give us everything we need
more abundantly than we ask or even think of asking.

For God's people   (from Colossians 1:3-13)

O God, Father of our Lord, Jesus Christ,
we thank you for your gifts to your people.
You called them into being, and gave them life
by creating them to your own image and likeness.
You call them to believe in your Son, Jesus Christ,
to hope for the reward which awaits them in heaven,
and to love others as you have loved them.

We pray that your good news,
the message of truth you revealed,
may spread through all the world and among all peoples,
so that it may help others as it has helped us.
For we heard your words and believed in your gifts,
and we have come to know them
by basing our actions on them,
and experiencing their value in our daily life.

So, Father, we never cease to pray for all christians,
that in the deepest wisdom and understanding,
they may know what pleases you and may always do it.

We pray that their lives and actions may be fruitful,
loving you and their friends
in the circumstances of life in which you placed them
so that the wisdom that flows from loving you
may help them to know you deeply and fully.

We pray for them, Father,
that strengthened by your glorious power,
they may never give in to temptation,
or fall or weaken under trials and persecution,
but bear with patient joy all you allow them to suffer.

We pray, Father, that they may always give you thanks
for allowing them to share the light of your glory
with us and all your people,
whom you rescue from the power of darkness,
and bring safely into the kingdom of your dear Son,
by whom we are set free, and our sins are forgiven.

Responding to Epistles

God's plan for Jesus (from Colossians 1:15-29)

Jesus, exact likeness of God whom we cannot see,
first-born in heaven, and first among all creatures,
through you and in you and for you
God created everything in heaven and on earth,
the people we can see and the angels we cannot see.
Before anything else existed, or anything was created,
you existed with God in the glory of the Trinity.
You give unity to all creatures, Lord Jesus,
for at the moment of creation
God planned all history to lead to you and flow from you.

To prepare for your coming, he chose and created
all people and things that existed before you came.
All that existed since, and that will exist till the end,
is changed by your coming and redemption.
As you are equal to the Father in the eternity of God,
so in time he planned you would be the first to rise,
to bring his whole world back to himself in you,
making peace through your death on the cross.

Help me, Lord Jesus, whenever I suffer,
that I may gladly help to complete your sufferings
that remain to be borne in your Body, the Church.
My sins have added to the world's suffering.
Make me happy to accept the trials and pain
which your love sees as my fair share of this suffering.
You made me your friend, Lord, to serve your church,
and to deliver God's message to all I am sent to:
family, children, friends, strangers, enemies.
This message was hidden for centuries since creation,
but now it is God's plan to make it known,
the glorious secret which gives us courage to live:
that you are in us and with us, O Lord Jesus Christ,
that we are called to share in the glory of God,
called to preach and teach and give good example,
and so bring all people to God in union with you.
Help me to toil and struggle for this work,
using your mighty power which is working with me.

Loving our neighbour   (from 1 John 3,5)

Father, you want us to believe in Christ your Son,
and to love one another as he has taught us.
My selfishness and the sinful example of the world
tells me to love myself, to look after myself,
and to forget my neighbour and his troubles.

O good Father in heaven, help me to know your love,
and the love of your Son, Jesus Christ,
so that, overcoming my selfishness and temptations,
I may always love and serve others.
You showed your love for us
by sending your Son to be the Saviour of the world.
Because you loved us so much,
we should surely love one another.
We believe in Jesus and confess he is your Son.
Therefore we know the love you have for us,
and we want to remain in your love
and be united to you forever.
We have never seen you,
but you are love,
and as long as we love one another,
you live in us, and your love is made perfect in us.

Father, whoever believes in Jesus is your child,
and whoever loves you will love your child also.
We are liars if we say we love you, Father,
while we refuse to love those who are your children.
If we do not love our brothers whom we see,
how can we love you whom we cannot yet see,
you who are our Father and theirs?

You gave us your commandments because you love us,
and we obey them because we love you.
Your commandments are not too hard for us
for, through our faith in Jesus Christ and his love,
we are able to defeat the world and our selfishness
which try to show us a different way.

PRAYERS OF SAINTS

All things made through Jesus (adapted from St Athanasius)

Jesus Christ, Lord and Saviour, Wisdom and Word of God,
your all-holy Father, beyond all created being,
our supreme steersman, acting as seems best to him
guides the world through you for our salvation.

The universe is good, for your Father made it good.
We see it as good, for he gave us the power to do so.
Its movements are neither meaningless nor haphazard,
because he created it with wisdom
arranging everything in complete and perfect order
so that you who govern and guide it
can be none other than the Word of God.

Jesus Christ, the personal Word of the good Father,
you have made this universe and keep it in being,
and you protect and enlighten it in your wisdom.

Jesus Christ, good Word of the good Father,
you have established the order of all things,
uniting and harmonizing opposites into a single beauty.

Jesus Christ, one only-begotten good God,
proceeding from the Father as from the source of good,
you guide and contain the universe.

After making everything by you, his own eternal Word,
and after bringing it to existence in you,
God did not abandon it to be destroyed by accident,
or to fail through its own dependent nature
lest it run the risk of returning to nothing.

Your Father is God, and governs the whole world
through you, Jesus, his Word, who yourself are God.
So, enlightened by your leadership, providence and plan,
all created beings remain firm in you, O Word of God,
whose whole being comes from the Father.
All things are thus aided by you to exist,
and to be preserved lest they fall back to nothingness,
as they would do if you did not protect them.

Praising God (from St Augustine's *Confessions* 1:1)

Lord, you have given us minds to know and praise you,
Even though we are but a tiny part of your creation,
who know the shortness of our life,
and know our weakness and failures and sins,
we still desire to praise you,
and you make it delightful for us to praise you,
because you have made us for yourself, O Lord,
and our hearts will never rest until they rest in you.
And we who seek you will find you,
and we who find you will praise you.
Therefore, O Lord, let me seek you, calling on you.
Let me call on you, believing in you,
for you have been revealed to me, O Lord,
and I believe your Word and what he revealed
and call upon you in the faith you have given me
through the incarnation and redemption of your Son,
and the teaching of his Church.

I call upon you, Lord and praise you.
Though I know I cannot contain you in human words
— for nothing in this world can contain you,
who have made all things in the universe —
I must praise you, O Lord my God:

Most high, most good, most powerful, most almighty!
Most merciful, most just, most hidden, most present!
Stable and unknowable, most beautiful, most strong!
Unchangeable, yet changing all things in this world!
Never new, never old, but renewing all things in time!
Always in action and always at rest!
Supporting and filling and overshadowing all things!
Creating, nourishing and perfecting all you made!
Seeking, yet wanting nothing!
You love without pain, you repent without grief!
Angry, yet always calm, jealous but not upset,
you change your world, but never your plan!
Never needy, you are pleased with our works!

Augustine's resolution

Too late have I known you, O everlasting truth.
Too late have I known you,
O beauty always old and ever new.
You were within me and I looked for you elsewhere,
and in my weakness
I ran after the beauty in the things you made.
You were with me, and I was not with you.
The things you created kept me far from you.

You called.
You cried out and pierced my deafness.
I heard you, and believed in you.
You shone forth, and lifted my blindness:
I found you, and long for you.
You sent forth your sweetness,
I tasted you, and hunger after you.

And now my whole hope is in nothing else
but in your very great mercy, O Lord, my God.
For he does not really love you,
who loves anything else
which he does not love for your sake.

O Love, which always burns and never grows less,
true charity, my God, set me all on fire.
Give me what you command, and command what you wish.
All-powerful God, you care for each one of us,
as if you loved that one alone,
and you care for all, as if all were but one.

Things of this world pass away
and other things replace them.
But you never pass away, you never depart.
O God, our Father, supremely good,
beauty of all things beautiful,
to you we entrust all we have received from you,
through Jesus Christ our Lord.

Changed by your love (Thomas à Kempis, *Imitation of Christ* 3.5.1)

I praise you and thank you, O heavenly Father,
Father of my Lord Jesus Christ,
because of your love and care for me,
and especially for the times you have consoled me,
filling me with spiritual joy I did not deserve
and which I had no right to expect.

I bless and glorify you for evermore,
with your only-begotten Son
and the Holy Spirit, the Comforter,
for ever and ever.

O Lord God, my holy lover, when you come to my heart,
all that is within me is filled with joy.
For as yet I am weak in love and imperfect in virtue,
and I need to be strengthened and comforted by you
so that the joyful feeling of experiencing your love
may free me from sinful inclinations and vices
and make me better able to love you,
courageous to suffer and faithful to persevere.

Your noble love, Jesus, leads me to do great things
and to desire always the way that is more perfect.

Love always reaches up to you
and is not tied down by things of this world.
When I love I am always at liberty,
always free from earthly attractions
never ensnared with any worldly interest,
and never depressed by misfortune.

Nothing is sweeter than love of you, my good God —
nothing stronger, nothing wider, nothing more pleasant,
nothing higher or fuller or better in heaven or earth.
For all true love is born of you, my God,
and cannot rest save in you, above all created things.

Lord, I love you (Thomas à Kempis, *Imitation of Christ* 3.5.4)

Loving you, Lord, I rejoice, I run, I fly!
I am free, and cannot be tied down!
I give all for all, and have all for all,
for I rest in you, one supreme God above all,
from whom comes everything in this world that is good.
When I truly love you, I do not look at your gifts,
but give myself above all gifts, to you, the Giver!

My God, my Love, you are all mine and I am all yours!
Let me grow in your love, so that in my inmost heart,
I may learn how sweet it is to love you,
in ever reaching above myself in fullness of joy,
possessed by you, immersed in you, dissolved in you!

In love, I feel no burden, and think nothing of work,
and would gladly seek to do more than I can.

In love, I remain always awake and watchful,
never restrained by difficulties, or disturbed by fear,
never too tired to continue when weary.

Loving you, I am effective in decision and action,
sincere, holy, pleasant, attractive to others,
strong, patient, prudent, long-suffering, courageous.

In true love, I am considerate, humble and upright,
sober, chaste, steadfast, quiet,
never seeking myself, for selfishness destroys love,
never soft, frivolous, or intent on useless things,
but always keeping a guard over my senses.

In love, I see myself as you see me, ever-loving Lord,
respecting myself as you do, for I am your child,
but I know my sins as offences against your love,
for which I hope for your mercy and pardon.

In love, I thank you, I trust in you and hope in you,
even when I do not taste the joy of your sweetness,
for we cannot live in this world without some sorrow,
and in true love I must be ready to suffer
and accept your will, my beloved.

In love, I embrace everything difficult that comes to me,
and I will never let anything turn me away from you.

St Patrick's Breastplate   (adapted)

I call today on God, my Creator, Three in One.
I rise up today with the power of God directing me,
   the strength of God supporting me,
   the wisdom of God guiding me,
   the eye of God watching for me,
   the ear of God listening to me,
   the hand of God protecting me,
   the way of God made known to me,
   the shield of God defending me,
   the angels of God guarding me —
   against snares of devils, against temptation of vices,
   against inclinations of evil, against all who wish me harm.

I call into my life today:
   the power of Christ's incarnation,
   to help me bring God's love to the world;
   the power of Christ's baptism,
   to set me apart for God's work;
   the power of Christ's crucifixion,
   to encourage me to accept suffering;
   the power of Christ's burial,
   to separate me from worldly desires;
   the power of Christ's resurrection,
   to raise me from my sins to a new life;
   the power of Christ's ascension,
   to prepare me for my true home in heaven;
   the power of Christ's coming in judgement,
   to enable me to fulfil his plan for me.

Christ with me, Christ before me, Christ behind me,
Christ in me, Christ beneath me, Christ above me,
Christ on my right hand, Christ on my left hand,
Christ where I sit, Christ where I arise.

Christ in the heart of everyone who thinks of me,
Christ in the mouth of everyone who speaks of me,
Christ in every eye that sees me,
Christ in every ear that hears me.

Hymn to Christ (St Columba)

Christ, in thee I do believe,
thou who all our pains relieve.
Come, protect and help me, Lord,
while I labour for thy word.
Hasten to my help, I pray,
bear my burden every day.
Thou the maker of mankind,
place in heav'n for all men find.

Christ who loves the virgin choir,
Christ, Redeemer from hell-fire,
fount of wisdom, pure and clear,
in whose word we hope and fear.
Christ, our guard at hour of fight,
Christ, who made the world and light,
Christ, who crowns each conquering soul,
count us in the heav'nly roll.

God of Gods, eternal light,
Lord most high, most sweet, most bright;
God of patience, past all thought;
God, thou teacher of the taught.
God who hast made all that was,
past and present, thou the cause,
Father, for thy Son's dear sake,
guard the way that I shall take.

Glory be to God on high,
Lord of all things far and nigh,
giving living strength in strife,
giving dead your lasting life.
Honour to the only Son,
with the Father ever one,
and to Holy Spirit, blest
equal power and praise addressed.

(Mary Cusack, *Lyra Hibernica Sacra*, 1878 — adapted)

Daily Prayer (W.B.M. — adapted)

Hear, O Lord, Oh! hear I pray,
this my prayer to you each day.

O grant me, Lord, my daily bread,
for soul and body too,
that in all things thy holy will,
I may ever strive to do.
Teach me to love thee as I ought,
to love each person dearly bought,
the souls so eagerly you sought,
may they be ever true.

Give me the light to see my faults,
a healthy shame of sin;
an outward calm and peace of mind,
an honest hate within.

Maintain the eagerness of youth
with courage true as steel,
grant me patience — strength to kneel,
and bowing pray as sinner should,
to you, O Lord, O God of truth,
that I may trust in you and feel
by you I'm understood.

Make me cheerful, tender, kind,
with sense of humour too;
whatever else, by day or night,
grant, that in all I do,
I always keep before my eyes,
the vision of a destiny,
that bids me ever rise.

Give me the strength to serve my foes,
to hide their faults, to heal their woes,
Oh! God of all, who only knows,
between us, which is right.

The Blessed Eucharist

This section tries to help people to use more fully the time they spend with Jesus in the Eucharist.

So some reflections and prayers have been included for use before Mass. The Communion prayers may help people to pray more effectively at Communion time, especially while others are receiving Communion. The Prayers after Communion can also be used after Mass, by those who wish to wait on a little longer. Prayers for visits, Holy Hours, etc have also been included.

REFLECTIONS

'Do this in memory of me'

When friends meet, they often recall the happy moments they shared in the past, in order to experience again the happiness and joy of those days. If they have tape recordings or photos, they will share them so that they can more effectively bring the past to life for a few moments.

Christ lived in this world for a few years of its history. He met personally only some of the people of his country and time. But he wants to be the friend of each and every person at every place and at every moment of the world's history. Coming to each of us as a friend, he wants to recall for us the events of his life that proved his love for us. He wants us to relive them with him, to share them with him.

As friends of his, we also want to do this. We reread the Gospels, we visit the crib at Christmas, honour the crucifix on Good Friday, and try to express to Christ what we would have liked to express to him face to face had we lived through these events with him two thousand years ago. By ourselves we can do no more.

But Christ is God, and is not dependent on conversation, prayer, tape-recorder, or photo to recall the past. Through his power as God, he enables us to overcome space and time, and now makes present again the love he showed in his sacrifice on Calvary, so that we might relive this wonderful event with him. It is as though he asks us: 'Do you recall the day I died for you? I know you cannot do so perfectly in spite of Gospel or prayerbook, crucifix or stations, so here is my Mass — do this in memory of me — do this to proclaim my death until I come again — do this to relive with me, and with my mother and saints, the events and love of Calvary.'

At Mass we offer our love to God

God showed his love in creating us and calling us to the happiness he has planned for us. He desires our love in return, and commands us to love him. Christ told us that this is the first and most important rule of our life.

When we love someone, we can show it in words, by telling him so. We can also show it by giving him a gift, as valuable a gift as we can afford. But even when it is not very valuable in itself, a gift becomes valuable and pleasing when it is offered as a sign of our love.

When many people join to give a gift like this, one acts in the name of the others, and offers the gift in some kind of formal ceremony. He is their representative and they will try to be present to take part in the ceremony and to show it is theirs. In the past, when people wanted to show their love for God, they prayed to him and kept his law — and they also offered him gifts, such things as animals, wine, fruits. They could not 'hand over' these to God, as they could to a human person. Instead, a priest, acting in their name, placed them on a holy place called an altar. Sometimes, they killed or destroyed them first, to show that they were giving them up completely. These gifts had no value in themselves to God, for God had made them, and they belonged to him before they were offered. Their value came from the love people showed in offering them.

Mass is the gift that Christ gave us to offer to God, to show our love for him. But it is also really valuable and pleasing to God *in itself*, because the gift we offer is the wonderful gift of love which Christ offered on Calvary to redeem us.

Mass is a sign of our love

We offer the gift of the Mass to show our love for God. When we offer a gift to a friend, our gift shows the friendship we have in our hearts for him. It would be wrong for us to hate or despise him, and merely pretend to love him, when we offer the gift.

So also, it is wrong for us to offer Mass to God as a sign of our love, if we do not love him in our hearts, or if we really do not care whether we love him or not. This is also very foolish. For God knows everything. So, unlike a human friend, he knows whether we really love him or are only pretending.

We love God in prayer when we make acts of love, including adoration, thanks, sorrow and petition. We love God when we keep his commandments. We love God when we love others as he has loved us. When we offer Mass, we should promise God that we will love him in every way we can in our lives, and make serious plans to do so during the days ahead.

The gift we offer is the love of Christ. Our love can never be as good or perfect as Christ's love, and we will often fail in our daily lives. We often sin. We often refuse to love God. But God is merciful, and loves us in spite of our sins. He still wants us to offer Mass, to tell him through our Mass that we really want to love him, and to ask his help for the future.

Christ's love offered at Mass

Christ told us that the first and most important commandment is, 'Love the Lord your God with your whole heart and soul and mind and strength.' We know we often fail in this. We often refuse to love and obey God. When we do love him, our love is often half-hearted and weak. But Christ gives us the Mass so that, with him, we might offer as our own to God the most perfect act of love the world has ever known.

Christ redeemed us on the cross, by his perfect love and obedience to his Father's plan, in accepting his sufferings and death, and offering them in an atonement for our sins. This was the most perfect act of love.

It was also the most perfect proof of God's wonderful, infinite love and care for us. Any act of Christ could have redeemed us, since he is the Son of God, the Second Person of the Trinity. But he knew we were selfish and hard-hearted. He knew his death was required to show his love so clearly that we could overcome our selfishness and love him in return. 'Greater love has no man than this, that a man lay down his life for his friends.'

At Mass, when Christ becomes present under the appearance of bread and wine, we offer again to God, with Christ himself, the act of our redemption. Christ's act of love on Calvary is made actual and repeated in this place at the moment of the consecration. We join him in offering his love to the Father. We rejoice in his love, and promise our love in return.

Four ways of loving God

We show our love for God in prayer of adoration, thanksgiving, sorrow and petition. At Mass, we offer these prayers with Christ to God.

In adoration, we honour God in accepting that he is our creator, and that we, his creatures, depend on him at every minute of our life. Our adoration does not add anything to God's glory, but through it we are fulfilling the first need of our nature, and we are living as God wants us to live, in the truth of our dependence on him. At Mass we join our human adoration to the worship Jesus gave his Father, a worship really worthy of God.

When we remember God's goodness to us, we show our love by thanking him. Again, God does not need our thanks — but we need to thank him, for it is the duty and joy of our nature to do so. At Mass, we make Christ's love present on our altar, to offer God a thanksgiving worthy of him.

Our love must include sorrow for having sinned and refused to love God. At Mass, we join our sorrow to Christ's redeeming act of satisfaction for sin.

We ask favours of God, not to make known our needs to him, but to show our dependence, confidence and love. At Mass, Christ prays with us, and our prayer should be like his prayer during his passion: 'Father, grant this favour, let this trouble pass away; but let your will be done, not mine, because you know what is good for me, and desire it more than I do myself.'

Bread and wine changed into Christ

Christ changed bread and wine into his body and blood at the Last Supper. When he took bread in his hands and said: 'This is my body', he changed it into his body through his divine power. At the words, 'This is my blood', he changed into his blood the wine he had taken into his cup.

With the words, 'Do this in memory of me', he gave this same power to the apostles and their successors in his ministerial priesthood. Whenever priests use these words as Christ used them, his power is with them to change bread and wine into his body and blood. What was bread before, still looks like bread and tastes like bread; but it is no longer bread, but Christ. What was wine before, still has the taste, the colour and all the other appearances of wine, but it is no longer wine; it is Christ.

Christ's body is not alone under the appearance of bread; and Christ's blood is not alone under the appearance of wine. Christ is risen from the dead, never more to die. Where his body or his blood is present, he is present himself as a complete living person.

The appearances of bread and wine are not changed at the consecration. Our eyes still see the colour of bread and of wine. And our lips still feel the taste of bread and of wine. It is only through our faith in Christ's words, and not by anything we see or taste or feel, that we know Christ is present under the appearances of bread and wine which our senses perceive.

We need faith to know the Mass

The year before he died, Jesus taught, 'I am the bread of life, which came down from heaven; if anyone eats of this bread, he shall live forever; and the bread which I will give is my flesh, for the life of the world.'

Some of those present began to ask a very practical question — 'How can this man give us his flesh to eat?'

But Jesus did not change his words or weaken them in any way. He made his promise clearer for them by saying, 'He who eats my flesh and drinks my blood has eternal life, and I will raise him up at the last day. For my flesh is food indeed, and my blood is drink indeed. He who eats my flesh and drinks my blood lives in me, and I in him.'

Many of his followers found it hard to believe this, and said, 'This is a hard saying, who can listen to it?' Jesus knew that there were many who did not believe, but he did not change what he had said.

Even when they went away, and refused to follow him any more, Jesus, who loved and cared for each one of them, did not call them back and tell them that they misunderstood him. He let them go; and then asked the apostles: 'Will you also go?' Peter answered in words of faith we should make our own; 'Lord, to whom shall we go? You have the words of eternal life, and we believe and know that you are the Christ, the Son of God.'

Mass offered by double consecration

Christ could come to live in us, and become the food of our souls, by changing bread alone into himself, without using wine.

But he wanted also to enable us to offer his love on Calvary to his heavenly Father. To do this, he chose to become present under the appearance of bread with the words: 'This is my body', and under the appearance of wine with the words: 'This is the cup of my blood'. This was the action he chose in his wisdom, to make his act of love on Calvary present again at different moments of time, and to give all who are baptized the right to offer it to God with him.

In this action, which he told us to repeat, he reminds us of his death, which he wants to re-present for us. During his Passion, his blood flowed from his wounds, and was separated from his body at his death. So, by using the words 'This is my body', and 'This is my blood', to become present under the appearances of both bread and wine, he reminds us of his death.

The words we use at Mass do not of course really separate the body and blood of Christ, living now for ever. But they remind us of the separation which took place on Calvary when he died. They are a sign of his death. Christ uses these words to bring about what they remind us of, and make Christ's offering of love on Calvary really present again on our altar. Mass therefore is a 'sacrament', the sacrament of the Eucharist — one of the seven sacraments Christ left with his Church.

At the consecration of the Mass, we should join in spirit with Christ's wonderful offering. Through Christ's presence under the appearance of bread, and under the appearance of wine, his love on Calvary becomes present for us to offer to God.

Sharing the sacrificial feast

When someone gives us a present, it is natural and usual to show we are pleased by sharing it with them in some way — by listening to the music of a record together, or by enjoying together at least part of a gift like a box of chocolates.

We offer Christ and his love to his Father during Mass. God, our Father, is pleased, and offers Christ back to us to be united to us as he is to the Father himself. He gives Christ to us in a sacred feast in the form of food. When we eat the appearance of bread under which Christ is present, Christ unites himself to our soul. In this world, we can never fully understand Christ's union with us in Holy Communion, nor can we feel it, but we know it happens because of our faith in Christ's words, "He who eats my flesh and drinks my blood, lives in me and I live in him'.

We should repeat these words of Christ each time we go to Holy Communion. By thinking and praying about them, we will gradually come to understand them deeply and more personally.

Love desires union with the person loved. Holy Communion brings about our union with Jesus Christ and so it is the best act of love we can offer him.

Food of our souls

We should desire Holy Communion each time we offer Mass. If through laziness, or for no good reason, we refuse to receive Communion when we can, we are not sharing fully in our attendance at Mass.

Christ comes to us in the form of food. By this, he shows that he wants to be the spiritual 'food' of our souls. When we eat earthly food, it is changed into us, and becomes part of us. It gives us strength to work. It helps us to overcome sickness and remain healthy.

Christ said, 'If anyone eats this bread that I will give, he will live forever . . . My flesh is food indeed, and my blood is drink indeed . . .'

In Communion, Christ does for my soul what ordinary food does for my body. He unites himself to me, and keeps my life of union with him strong and healthy. He strengthens me to live for him. He helps me to overcome and avoid the sickness of sin.

He comes to me, and loves all others from within me. He comes to others who receive him, and loves me from within their souls. So, I should love all others with him when I go to Communion and I should allow others to love and help me.

His love for each one of us, which we share in Holy Communion, is such a valuable gift that in comparison, all differences between us become unimportant.

Mass ratifies our covenant

God promised the children of Abraham that he would be their God and they would be his people. They promised they would honour him as their God, accepting all the duties of being his people.

This was the promise, the agreement, the contract, the testament, the covenant under which Jews were to live until the Saviour came. Sometimes they were faithful, sometimes unfaithful. But God was always faithful, and protected his people for centuries, preparing for Christ's coming.

During the history of the Jewish people, God commanded them to recall his plan of salvation, especially the important historical events through which he showed his love. They celebrated their feasts by reading the biblical records of these events, and performed actions that symbolized them. Thus they entered into them in spirit and imagination and prayed and acted as they would have done had they been present in reality.

On Calvary, as God and Man, Christ ratified his new covenant for us in his blood, when he restored us to a new friendship with the Father.

Christ gave us the Mass, so that we can relive our redemption, not merely in spirit, but in reality; so that we, God's people in his Church, can effectively ratify our covenant with God at this moment and in this place, by making present the same act that Christ offered once on Calvary. At each Mass we attend God renews his acceptance of Calvary and we can renew our personal covenant with him, and get his help to live it each day.

Mass, our offering for the Lord's Day

Christ himself offers each Mass through the words of the priest. As we are members of Christ, united to him through Baptism, we can really and truly offer the Mass with him. The Mass is ours because we are baptized. An unbaptized person, even though present at Mass, does not offer the Mass with Christ. He has no right to claim it as 'his'.

If we realize that the Mass is *our* offering, we will understand that it is a great privilege to be present at Mass, and to take our full part in offering it with Christ to God. We will be especially careful to offer our Mass every Sunday.

God wants us to live in this world until we die. But he does not want us to grow so fond of it that we forget him and our true home in heaven. God made us, and he knows that we need one day each week to leave aside all unnecessary work, and to remember and honour him. His law, therefore, tells us that we need to keep one day holy each week, that one day in seven be given to God.

The apostles chose Sunday to be the day given to God each week. No Catholic can say he keeps Sunday holy, if he refuses without reason to come and offer Christ's act of love to God. That is why the Church's law commands us to attend Mass each Sunday.

If we offer Mass faithfully Sunday after Sunday, God will become the most important reality in our lives, and the rest of our lives will fall into proper place. Unless he is 'Number One', through regular Sunday Mass, our lives will turn 'upside down', and we will find it difficult not to fall away from him into a life of sin.

We offer Mass together

The Mass is not yours alone, or mine alone. It belongs to the whole Church. You or I never offer it alone, but united to the other members of the people of God. We must be ready and glad to join with those of them who are at Mass with us, in the prayers, songs and actions of the Mass, so that our union and love in offering Mass together will continue to bind us together in our lives outside Mass.

Together we will listen reverently to the word of God during the first part of Mass, to see what lesson God has for us, and to see how we can practise it in our daily lives.

Together we should listen to the prayers the priest offers in our name, and all together be ready to answer 'Amen' loudly when he is finished. 'Amen' means, 'So be it', 'Yes, Lord that's my prayer'.

We should not be lazy. At times we will sing out our prayers and hymns strongly with all our fellow-parishioners. At other times we will pray reverently with our bodies, standing, kneeling and sitting, with our minds fixed on the offering we are making. We will use periods of silence for our own personal prayers to God or Jesus Christ. If we deliberately talk or play or look around us without any reason, we hurt ourselves; and we also hurt those near us by making it harder for them to keep their minds on God's love during Mass.

A full parish church every Sunday, with all united in love, through prayer, song and action, gives witness to Christ's love, and helps others to recognize and love him with us.

PRAYERS BEFORE MASS

Christ is coming

O Lord Jesus Christ, Son of God,
you are coming in the name of the Lord.
You are coming to be with us.

You are coming to offer sacrifice for us.
You are coming to show your love for us.
You are coming to show forth to us,
your people in this sinful world,
the death you offered for us on Calvary.

You are coming, to change our gifts
into your body and blood,
and to put this offering of yours
into our hands that it may also be ours.
You are coming to remind us of your love,
to show us your love,
and to offer it once more for us from this world:

Your coming will be useless for me, Lord,
unless my faith is strong.
Lord, strengthen my faith:
you have the words of eternal life,
and I have believed and come to know,
that you are the Christ, the Son of God.

I can see with my eyes the signs you choose,
the bread and wine prepared for our sacrifice.
But these are useless, unless you come to us,
to change them into yourself.

Through your power you will be present —
through my faith, I will know you are here.
Through your presence, the Mass is living —
through my faith, it is alive and real for me.
Through your presence, you offer the Mass —
through my faith and baptism, I offer it with you.

Act of love

O God, my Father, you loved me from eternity,
and therefore you chose me and created me.
In each event of history, at each moment of time,
you knew that your love would be effective,
that I would be conceived and born as you had planned,
and that I would find myself living here, and now,
able to give you my heart's love, weak though it is,
in return for your infinite love.
Your Son, Jesus Christ, has revealed that you created me
because you love me
and want me to share your life and happiness.

Father, I want to love you with all my heart and soul
as long as I live, both here and in heaven.
Loving you is my true life and my true happiness.
Nothing else will really make me happy.
My God, I want to be yours, I want to belong to you.
I want to be united to you, now and forever.
I want to enjoy your friendship
and to share your life
both here in this world where I know you by faith,
and in heaven where I will see you face to face,
and know you as you know me.

I love you, I promise to obey you and serve you.
I will love and help others for your sake.
Because I love you, I will gladly keep your commands.
You gave them to me to show me the best way to live
and to guide me to happiness here and in heaven.
But my love is weak and I often sin through weakness,
in pride, envy, laziness, lust, hatred, anger, gluttony.
Forgive me. Strengthen me. Help me to love you.
Jesus Christ alone loved you perfectly.
When he died for us, in obedience to your will,
his act of love was most pleasing to you.
His love is now mine to offer you at this Mass.
I offer it to you gladly.

Knowing and loving God

Lord God, heavenly Father,
all things were made by you and for you.
You love the human race
more than any of your earthly creatures.
To us alone you gave powers of knowing and loving.

O God, our first duty is to know you,
and to use our freedom to love you.
My love for you is my own; it is mine alone to give.
Many people love you far more than I do,
but no one can give the love of my soul except myself.
If I refuse, this love will not be given by anyone.
Look kindly on me whom you created in love.
Help me to adore you in spirit and truth,
that I may love you with all my strength.

You love members of your Church in a special way.
You have told us about your love for each one of us.
You have called us to the happiness of heaven.
We thank you because after our sin,
you rescued us from the power of darkness,
and led us into the kingdom of your beloved Son,
who brought us redemption and forgiveness,
giving us new life, through water and Spirit.
We offer you this Mass in love and thanksgiving.

Lord God, heavenly Father,
you redeemed and sanctified us through Christ.
You made us a chosen people, a kingly priesthood,
a community called to be holy in you.
You gave us power to offer your sacrifice.
Grant through our Mass today,
that we may love you with all our heart and soul,
that we may be willing to do your will,
that we may love and help our neighbours,
and be willing to sacrifice time, effort and money
to make them happy, both here and in eternity.

Proclaiming Christ's death

In his love and power, Jesus changes bread and wine
into the body that was given for us,
and the blood that was shed for us.
Therefore, Father, as often as we eat "this bread",
and drink "the chalice" at our Mass,
we are privileged to proclaim in this sinful world,
the death of the Lord Jesus until he comes;
this also is the privilege of our whole life:

"What death do we proclaim, at Mass and in our lives?"
Jesus loved us and gave himself up for us,
as a pleasing sacrifice to you, his Father.
Let us walk in love, as he has loved us.
Let us show forth his love to our world,
by the goodness and sacrifice of our lives.

"What death do we proclaim, at Mass and in our lives?"
Jesus died for sins, once for all.
He, the holy and good, died for us sinners,
that he might bring us to you, who are our God.
O Father, as he has loved and forgiven us,
help us to love and serve others,
forgiving our enemies,
and showing by our love that we are his followers.

"What death do we proclaim, at Mass and in our lives?"
Humbling himself, Jesus became obedient to death,
even to death on a cross.
Let us show forth our love, O loving Father,
by doing your will and obeying your commands.

"What death do we proclaim, at Mass and in our lives?"
Though Jesus had joy set before him with you,
he endured the cross, despising the shame.
Let us live in patience and perseverance, Father,
the lives you plan for us in this world,
loving you, and helping everyone we meet,
and making your world a better place to live in
until we come to share your life and joy in heaven.

Offering Christ's love

Lord Jesus, as the first rule for our life,
you told us to love God with our whole heart and soul.
But you knew, only too well,
that we would never love him as we should,
or serve him as he deserved to be served.
So, in your goodness and mercy,
you enabled us to offer again with you to God,
your infinite act of love on Calvary.

Soon, at the consecration of this Mass,
you will be present under the appearance of bread
through the words, "This is my body";
and you will be present under the appearance of wine
through the words, "This is the cup of my blood,
the blood of the new and everlasting covenant."

I know you are risen from the dead,
never more to die.
So your body and blood can never more be separated.
By the words, "This is my body". "This is my blood",
you remind us of your death on the cross
where your body and blood were really separated,
and you died on the cross.
At Mass, through this sacramental action,
you now enable us to offer again with you
your gift of love on Calvary
to your heavenly Father.

As you changed bread and wine
into your body and blood,
offering yourself in love to your Father,
I offer with you the love of your whole life.
With it I offer my own weak love.
Through you and with you may I love God more.
May my life become more like yours in loving him.

I offer myself

We will bring bread and wine to your altar, Lord,
signs of our daily life and work.
All our thoughts, words, actions should be yours.
We offer them to you, with this bread and wine.
You are our creator, we belong to you.
We freely give back what you first gave us.
We offer you our love, service and obedience.
We want to serve you, and to do your will.

As one of your people, I offer myself to you.
Accept my body, that it may serve you,
with all its weakness and with its strength.
You have made it for eternal glory.
Let it not be led by earthly feelings alone.
Keep it healthy and strong, to work for you,
and for the happiness of others.

Accept the soul you gave me, and all its powers.
Let my thoughts and hopes be devoted to you.
Keep away from me all useless distractions.
Accept my heart with its desires and feelings,
with its love and its sufferings,
with its troubles and its joys.
Make me pure and good as you desire me to be.
Keep me from loving myself in selfishness.
Help me to love and help others as you do.
Accept the good I have done or have wanted to do,
all my work and efforts, my cares and sorrows.
Accept what is imperfect and bad in me —
May it help me to know my weakness and need of you.

Jesus, when you change my gifts into yourself,
to become my perfect gift to the Father,
change what is bad in me into good
so that my life may become a more worthy gift
to be offered with you to God.

PRAYERS BEFORE COMMUNION

Bread of life   (John 6)

Lord Jesus, because of your love for us,
you became man with a human body like ours.
You came from heaven, not to do your will,
but to do the will of him who sent you.
You loved us even to death,
and washed us in your blood.

In this sacrifice of the Mass,
you have again offered yourself and your love,
to the Father for us;
In the sacrament of your love, you remain with us,
and give yourself to us as food.

Lord Jesus Christ, you are the Bread of Life.
Whoever comes to you will not hunger.

Lord Jesus Christ, the bread that you give us
is your flesh for the life of the world.
He who eats your flesh and drinks your blood,
will have everlasting life,
and you will raise him up on the last day.

For your flesh is truly food,
and your blood is truly drink.
When I eat your flesh and drink your blood,
I live in you and you live in me.
As the heavenly Father lives in you,
and you live in him,
so too I who eat your flesh will live for ever.
He who comes to you will never hunger,
he who believes in you will never thirst.
You have the words of eternal life.

We believe and we know
that you are the Christ, the Son of God,
and believing, we will have life in your name.

Faith in your presence   (Thomas à Kempis, *Imitation of Christ* 4.1)

'Come to me you who labour and are heavy burdened,
and I will give you rest.'
'The bread that I will give is my flesh
which I gave so that the world may live.'

'Whoever eats my flesh and drinks my blood
lives in me, and I live in him.'
'The words I have spoken to you
are spirit and truth.'

These are your words, Lord Jesus Christ,
though not all spoken at one time,
nor written in one place.

They are yours, because you have spoken them.
They are also mine, given by you for my salvation.
I gladly receive them from your mouth,
so that they may be firmly rooted in my heart.
Even though my sinfulness makes me slow to receive you,
your tender words of sweetness and love encourage me.

You command me to approach you with confidence
if I desire to be one with you,
and to receive the food of immortal life
if I desire to reach everlasting life and glory.

'Come, all you who are weary and burdened,'
you say to me, 'and I will give you rest.'

O sweet and loving word in the ear of a sinner
that you, O Lord my God invite the poor and needy
to the Communion of your most holy body.
How shall I dare to approach
who am conscious of no good on which I can presume?
How shall I introduce you into my house,
who have so often offended your most loving goodness?
Yes! the heavens of heaven cannot contain you
and yet you say, 'Come you all to me!'
Unless you, O Lord, did indeed say this,
who would believe it to be true?
Unless you commanded it, who would dare approach?

Come Lord Jesus

Prayer of desire

Jesus Christ, I want you
I want you for my own sake,
   because I am so weak,
   because I am a sinner,
   because I am nothing.

I want you for your sake,
   so that I may know you,
   so that I may love you,
   so that I may become like you.

I want you for the sake of others,
   so that I may never do harm to them,
   so that I may always do good to them,
   so that I may give you to them.

Jesus Christ, I believe that you want me
You want me for my sake,
   because you made me,
   because you died for me,
   because you love me.

You want me for your own sake,
   that I may be your joy,
   that I may be your crown,
   that I may be one with you.

You want me for the sake of others,
   that through me you may help others,
   that through me you may teach others,
   that through me you may come to them.

I am not worthy (Thomas à Kempis, *Imitation of Christ* 4.2)

Jesus, trusting in your goodness and great mercy,
I come sick to my Saviour,
hungry and thirsty to the Fountain of life,
poor and needy to the King of heaven,
a servant to my Lord, a creature to my creator,
and one in trouble to my loving comforter.

But how can this happen, that you should come to me?
Who am I, that you should give yourself to me?
Lord Jesus, you know me, your servant,
and you know that of myself I am nothing,
nothing by which I would deserve that you come to me ...
I confess therefore my unworthiness,
I acknowledge your generosity,
I praise your goodness,
and I thank you for your wonderful love.
For it is for your own sake you do this,
not on account of my merits;
and so, your goodness becomes clearer to me
and your love is poured out more abundantly,
and your humility shines out more brightly.
Since then it has pleased you to make this decision,
and you have planned this gift for my welfare,
I also am pleased and rejoice at your merciful love,
and pray that my sinfulness may not be an obstacle.

But what shall I think about in this communion,
as I approach you whom I can never worthily adore
but whom I still desire to receive with love?
Nothing is better or more useful for me
than to humble myself entirely before you,
and to praise your infinite goodness above me ...
I proclaim you as my Lord and God,
and I praise your holy name for ever.
Lord, I am not worthy that you should come to me;
say only the word, and my soul will be healed.

Prayers before Communion

I praise your love (Thomas à Kempis, *Imitation of Christ* 4.2)

Lord Jesus Christ, you are the Saint of saints
and I am your sinful creature, your ungrateful friend!
I am not worthy even to look up towards you!
And yet, you come to me, and wish to be with me.

You want to give me heavenly food,
the bread of angels,
no other indeed, than yourself, the living Bread,
who came down from heaven and gives life to the world.

This is your gift from which your love is poured out,
and from which your goodness shines for all to see.
I praise you for ever for your goodness and love.
How amazing your plan for giving us the Eucharist!
and how wonderfully you carried it out!
How admirable is your work, Lord Jesus Christ,
how mighty your power, how certain your truth!
For you have spoken and all things were made
and that which you commanded, was done.

It is indeed a wonderful truth, known only by faith,
beyond the understanding of our human minds,
that you, O Lord my God, true God and man,
are contained entire under a small form of bread,
and are eaten by your friends, without being consumed.
You are the Lord of all, and in need of no one,
yet in this sacrament you want to dwell in us.
Keep me safe and pure and good,
so that I may often be able to receive this gift
which you left for your honour and perpetual memorial.

I rejoice and I thank you for this noble gift
for as often as I offer Mass and receive Communion,
it should be for me as great, as new, as delightful,
as if you, Lord Jesus Christ, that very day
descended to the virgin's womb and were made man,
or, hanging on the Cross, died for our salvation.
For your charity, Lord Jesus, is never diminished,
and the greatness of your love is never exhausted.

Lord, forgive me (Thomas à Kempis, *Imitation of Christ* 4.9)

Lord, all things in heaven and on earth are yours.
I desire to give myself freely to you
and to remain for ever yours.

Lord, with sincere heart I offer myself to you today,
to be your servant for ever more,
and to glorify and praise you for ever.

Receive me with the offering of your precious Body,
which I offer you today on your holy altar
in the presence of your invisible angels,
for my salvation and the salvation of all your people.

Lord, I offer you on this altar,
all the sins which I have committed in your sight.
Forgive me for my failures against you,
and restore me to your life and love,
fully pardoning me and receiving me back in mercy.

Forgive me, O my God, forgive my sins,
for the sake of your holy Name.
Save my soul,
which you have redeemed with your precious blood.
I offer myself to your mercy.
I commit myself into your hands.
Deal with me according to your goodness,
and not according to my wickedness and sin.
I offer you also all my good works and actions
few and imperfect though they may be.
Lord, correct them, improve them and sanctify them.

I offer my prayers and this Eucharist
for all those who have asked my prayers,
for all those who have injured or hurt me
and those whom I have ever hurt or led into sin.
Lord, forgive us all our sins,
and heal the hurt we have done to one another.
Take, O Lord from our hearts
all suspicion, anger and pride,
all that wounds charity and lessens brotherly love.

Prayers before Communion

I need your love (Thomas à Kempis, *Imitation of Christ* 4,16)

O most sweet and most loving Lord Jesus Christ,
whom I now desire to receive with joyful love,
you know my weakness, and the pressures I endure.
You know how strong are my vices,
and how often I am troubled and tempted.

To you, and you alone, I come to be cured;
I speak to you who know all things,
to whom my whole interior personal life is clear,
and who alone can perfectly comfort and assist me.
For you know the good things I stand most in need of,
and how poor I am in virtue and good deeds and love.

Behold, Lord, I stand before you, poor and naked,
begging grace and imploring mercy.
Feed your hungry beggar,
inflame my coldness with the fire of your love,
enlighten my blindness with the light of your presence.
Help me to measure earthly created things by your life,
and value them by the light of your teaching and love.

Make me patient in all suffering and pain.
Raise up my heart to you into heaven.
Do not allow me to wander from you on earth.
May you alone be delightful to me for the rest of my life.
For you alone are my meat and drink,
my love and my joy, my sweetness and my whole good.
May your presence completely inflame and consume me,
and change me into yourself, that I may be made one with
you by your gift of spiritual union
and by the melting of your burning love.

Do not let me be still hungry and dry when I leave,
but deal with me in your mercy,
as you have often dealt wonderfully with your saints.
I pray that I may be completely set on fire by you,
and die to myself and my sinful desires,
since you are a fire always burning and never-failing,
a love to purify hearts and enlighten minds.

PRAYERS AFTER COMMUNION OR AFTER MASS

O Jesus, hidden God   (Fr Rawes OSC)

O Jesus, hidden God, I cry to thee;
O Jesus, hidden Light, I turn to thee;
O Jesus, hidden Love, I run to thee;
O Jesus, deathless Love, I live for thee;
With all the strength I have I worship thee;
With all the love I have I cling to thee;
With all my soul I long to be with thee,
And fear no more to fail, or fall from thee.

White-robed, blood-sprinkled Jesus, come to me;
Thou who didst die for longing love for me,
Thou King in all thy beauty, come to me,
And go no more away, dear Lord, from me,
O God, most beautiful, most priceless One;
O God, most glorious, uncreated One;
O God, immense, O God, the living One;
Thou ever-loved and ever-loving one.

Make me, O holy God, thy treasured one;
Make me, O glorious Love, thy precious one,
Make me, O blessed Light, thy chosen one;
Make me for evermore thy loving one.
My soul is dark away from thee, my own!
My eyes are dim in seeking thee, my own!
My heart leaps up with joy to thee, my own!
My spirit faints receiving thee, my own!

Thou art my all, and I love none like thee;
With all my heart I give myself to thee,
and waiting wait, O King and Spouse, for thee,
Till I am one for evermore with thee;
O sweetest Jesus, bring me home to thee;
And free me, dearest Lord, from all but thee,
Unloose all chains that keep me back from thee.
Call me, O thrilling Love, I follow thee.

O hidden Love, who now art loving me,
O wounded Love, who once wast dead for me,
O risen Love, who art alive for me,
O patient Love, who weariest not of me —
O bear with me till I am lost in thee!
O bear with me till I am found in thee!
O bear with me till I am one with thee
For evermore in life of Trinity.

Food of the hungry   (Smyltan — adapted)

Food of the hungry, hope of the sad!
Rest of the weary, bliss of the glad!
Life for the lifeless, strength of the weak!
Joy of the joyless, crown of the meek!

Food for the angels, manna from heaven!
Comfort of mortals, life-giving leaven!
Pardon of sinners, seeking their home!
Guide to all wand'rers, ceasing to roam.

Pledge of salvation, refuge in death!
Sacred oblation, sign of our faith!
Peace to our troubled, tempest-tossed mind!
Healing for wounded, eyes to the blind!

Hail! Son of Mary, sacrifice pure!
Hail! we implore thee, keep us secure,
filled with thy mercy, sharing thy light,
hoping for glory, evermore bright.

Prayer of praise

Lord Jesus Christ, I praise you.
Light of the world, I worship you.
You are in me and I am in you.
My Lord and my God.

I worship you, my Saviour.
Jesus, I want to live for you.
Jesus, I am willing to die for you.
Jesus, I am yours in life and in death.
Jesus, I am yours. Yours I will remain.
I love you forever, my Lord and my God.
God most holy, God most holy and strong.
God most holy and strong and immortal.
You hold the world in your hands.
In your hands I am safe.

Lord, you are the one I trust.
You are the king of the world.
You are the joy of angels and saints.
You are the strength of Christians.
You are the light that never fails.
Stay with me, Lord Jesus,
I want to become like you.
I want to please you always,
I want to love everyone for your sake,
for we are all united in your love.

You are the vine and we are the branches.
We will indeed bear fruit if we remain in you.
We show our love by keeping your commandments.
Bring all men to believe in you and love you.
May your kingdom come.
Your life comes from the Father.
Our life comes from you.
Lord, show us the Father.
Lead us into your glorious kingdom.

Humility and confidence

Father in heaven, in this Mass and Communion
you have given me your Son, Jesus Christ,
because you know that I need him and his love.
You have given him, not because I deserve it,
but because I am weak.
You choose the foolish of the world
to shame the wise,
and what is weak in the world to shame the strong,
to bring to nothing what the world thinks important,
so that nobody might boast in your presence.
For the wisdom of this world is folly with you,
and I must become a fool in the eyes of the world
in order to become truly wise.

My strength comes from you, my God, not from myself.
You are the source of my life in Christ Jesus,
for you gave him to me as my Way, my Truth, my Life.
When I am united to Christ, I have everything,
everything in the world, and life and death
and the present and the future,
for I belong to Christ, and Christ belongs to you.

I must not be proud of myself, or of what I do.
I have nothing that I have not received.
I should not boast of anything as if it were my own.
I thank you, and praise you for all you have given.
Everything I do,
whether I eat or drink or work or play,
I will do for your glory, praising and thanking you.
Make me humble in mind and act, like Jesus, your Son.
He was God, but he was willing to empty himself.
Becoming man and taking the form of a servant,
he humbled himself, and became obedient unto death,
death on a cross.
Make me humble and obedient like him.

How I should love

You have come to give me your love, Lord Jesus,
so that I may love you and my neighbour.
If I lose your love, I have nothing.
I cannot love you without loving my neighbour.

May my love for you and my fellow men
make me patient and kind.
May it prevent me from being jealous or proud,
boastful or insolent.
Make my love so strong, Lord Jesus,
that I do not insist in having my own way;
that I be not angry or brood over injuries;
that I do not rejoice at wrongdoing,
but rejoice at the victory of truth.
Through my love for you and my neighbour,
may I bear all things, may I believe all things,
may I hope all things, may I endure all things.

Help me to lead a life worthy of your love
with humility, meekness, self-control, and mercy,
eager to preserve the unity the Spirit gives,
united to everyone in peace and love.

Help me to work with the gifts you have given me
for the building up of your body, Jesus Christ,
till in you we reach unity of faith and knowledge.
May we all grow in your Church, Lord Jesus,
to the maturity of your fullness.
May we no longer be like children,
led astray by the cunning and lies of wicked men
and foolishly accepting every change of doctrine.
Love must be our whole aim,
for love never ends, but lives on in heaven,
where we will be united to you, face to face,
for ever and ever in your love.

Holiness of life (St Thomas Aquinas)

O merciful God,
help me to do your will perfectly in all things.
May I long to work only for your honour and glory.
May I rejoice in nothing except what leads to you.
May I desire nothing that leads away from you.

May all sinful things be as nothing in my eyes.
May all that is yours be dear to me,
and may you, Lord, be dear to me above all things.
May I desire nothing apart from you.
May all joy have no importance for me without you.
May all effort and work delight me
when it is for you.

Make me, O Lord, obedient without complaint,
poor without regret, patient without murmur,
humble without pretence,
joyful without foolishness,
and truthful without disguise.

Give me, O God, an ever-watchful heart,
which nothing can ever draw away from you.
Give me a noble heart,
which no unworthy love can ever drag down to sin.
Give me an upright heart, which no evil can bend.
Give me an unconquerable heart,
which no trouble can crush or overcome.
Give me a heart full of love for you,
which no evil love can steal for itself.

Give me, O God, understanding to know you,
perseverance to seek you and wisdom to find you.
Give me a life which will please you,
and a hope which will unite me to you when I die.

Prayer of trust (Cardinal Newman)

In your love, my God, you have chosen and created me
to do you some definite service.
You have given some work to me,
which you have not given to any other.
I have my place in your plan.
I may never know what it is in this life,
but I will be told it in the next.

Therefore, I will trust you in all things.
If I am sick, my sickness can serve you.
If I am worried, my worry can serve you.
If I am in sorrow, my sorrow can serve you.
You do nothing in vain; you know what you are doing.
You may take away my friends,
you may put me among strangers,
you may make me feel forgotten,
you may make my spirits sink,
you may hide my future from me —
still, you know what you are doing, and I trust you.

For peace of heart (Cardinal Newman)

Most sacred, most loving Heart of Jesus,
hidden in the Holy Eucharist,
you beat for us still.
You say, as you said when you lived,
'My delight is to be with the children of men.'

When you come to live within me,
make my heart beat with your Heart.
Make my soul free from all that is earthly,
all that is hard and cruel,
all that is proud and sensual,
all badness, disorder and death.

Fill my heart with your presence,
so that nothing can disturb me,
and that in your love and your fear,
I may have peace.

Praying with Christ's Friends

Lord Jesus, you offer your love on our behalf,
by changing bread and wine into yourself.
Change me, too, and my whole life,
so that I may love you as you want me to do.
Make me pure and good, faithful and devoted,
careful of my duties to you, and to others.

Help me to remember heaven always.
Through your coming, you are close to me,
as your friends were close to you,
when you lived among them.
They knew and loved you whom they saw,
I have not seen you, but I believe in you;
I know and love you through faith,
and through the prayers and love
my faith enables me to offer to you.

I pray to you in the words used by those
who came to you for help and forgiveness
while you were on earth:—

O God, be merciful to me, a sinner.
You can make me clean.
You who take away the sins of the world,
have mercy on me.
Lord, I have sought you sorrowing,
to whom shall I go?
You have the words of eternal life,
and I have believed and have known,
that you are the Christ the Son of God,
you who are come into this world.
I know that you know all things,
and I believe that you came out from God.
Master, I will follow you wherever you go.
I will lay down my life for you.
Lord, you know all things, you know that I love you.

PRAYERS BEFORE THE BLESSED SACRAMENT

At the consecration of Mass, bread and wine are changed into the Body and blood of Jesus Christ. He is then present on the altar under the appearance of bread and wine until received by his people in Holy Communion. Between Masses he remains present in our tabernacles in this same way: having come under the appearance of bread at a previous consecration, he remains until he is received in future Holy Communions of his people.

So, when we follow a long-standing Catholic prayer-custom of visiting him in his tabernacle, we can well use the thoughts and prayers the Church puts before us in her Eucharistic Prayers — especially the prayers after the consecration, when in worshipping God, we pray with Christ, who, before us on the altar, has offered himself for our redemption, and is waiting for us to receive him in Holy Communion. Visits, Exposition and Benediction can thus prolong our presence at Mass; they can continue and extend the offering and thanksgiving of our last Mass, and help us prepare for our next.

'Public and private devotion to the Holy Eucharist outside Mass is also highly recommended: for the presence of Christ, who is adored by the faithful in the Sacrament, derives from the Sacrifice, and is directed towards sacramental and spiritual Communion.'
(Pope John Paul II, in *Inaestimabile Donum*, para. 20, 3 April 1980.)

Prayers before the Blessed Sacrament

The prayers that follow have been based on Eucharistic Prayers, — but the words are here addressed directly to Jesus, rather than to the Father as in Mass. And also they have been written in the first person singular, to make them more personal to the one using them.

Friendship and unity (Eucharistic Prayer for Reconciliation I, adapted)

As I now kneel in your presence, I recall your love.
I celebrate your death and resurrection,
and I look forward to the day you will return
to take me to the full joy of your Father's home.

Lord Jesus, you restored us to God's friendship
by your sacrifice on the cross.
Bring us back also to friendship with one another.
You have called us to share in your sacrifice.
By the power of your Holy Spirit,
make us one body, healed of all divisions.

As we each grow in love for you,
keep us all united in mind and heart
with... our Pope and with... our bishop.
Unite us in your love, Lord Jesus,
to work together for the coming of your Kingdom
until, united to you, our Redeemer and Brother,
we will share the life of the Trinity,
joining you in praising and thanking your Father
in the happiness of heaven, for ever and ever.

Offering Christ's love (Eucharistic Prayer I, adapted)

I come before you, Lord Jesus Christ,
to remember and celebrate your love —
your love for God, your love for us your people,
your obedience to God's plan for our welfare,
which you showed by dying to save us,
and renewed in the Mass that left you here.

As your Father has chosen me to love and serve him,
I take you as my model, and your life as my guide.
I remember that you suffered and died to redeem me,
that you rose from the dead to give me life,
that you ascended into heaven to wait for me,
that you will take me to the Father when I die.

Your Father, our God of glory and majesty,
is also our Father, who gives us many gifts.
His greatest gift is one we can offer back to him,
the holy and perfect sacrifice of the Mass,
which you offer your Father on our behalf,
under the appearance of bread and wine.
I ask God, your Father and ours, to accept it,
as he accepted human gifts from men in the past,
the offering of Abel and Abraham,
and that of Melchisedech, a Gentile stranger.

I can offer this gift with you, Jesus my brother,
for I am united to you through my baptism.
I now hope and pray that you strengthen that union,
as I come before you in love, faith and prayer.
With you, I now offer again your wonderful love,
which in heaven, you eternally offer your Father,
and which is being renewed at this very moment
somewhere in our world of time and space.

Prayers before the Blessed Sacrament

Prayer for others (Eucharistic Prayer I, adapted)

Lord, I pray for the dead,
especially those I personally knew in this life,
friends whom I loved and who loved me,
people whom I hurt, or who hurt me.
Lord, I thank them for all the good they have done.
I forgive them any hurt they gave me,
just as I know that, united to you in heaven,
they forgive me whatever hurt I gave them.
I am glad to accept the sufferings that come to me —
as my proper share of the suffering caused by sin,
by my sins and by the sins of others.

I pray for all who have gone before me,
all those marked with your sign of faith in baptism,
called to union with you in this life and the next.

I pray that through you and with you and in you,
they may find light, happiness and peace,
sharing your hidden life in the Blessed Trinity
with the Father and Spirit in never-ending love.

I pray for my friends still living in this world
for those who asked or need my prayers…
for those whom I meet every day…
for those who have hurt me or offended me…
for all still struggling to love you in this life.

I look forward to meeting them all in heaven,
and all the martyrs who have died for you,
and all the saints who have lived for you,
and everyone who has died in your love.
With all your saints who now know you face to face,
I renew my love for you, whom I know by faith.

Trust, praise and peace (Eucharistic Prayer I, adapted)

Lord Jesus, I believe in your living presence here.
I hope in the promises of happiness you have made.
Though I have sinned, I trust in your Father's mercy
which you have revealed to me.
I trust that he will not treat me as I deserve,
but will forgive me because of your death for me
and his love for you whom he sent to save me.

Through you, our Lord Jesus Christ,
the Father gives all his gifts to his people
especially his sacraments of love and reconciliation.
Through you he fills them with life for us.
Through you he blesses them and makes them holy.

So, also, it is through you, and with you, and in you
that I can offer to my almighty and eternal God,
whom you have made known to me as my Father,
all the praise and honour and glory I owe him,
using now the words that you taught us to say:
'Our Father who art in heaven...'

Because of your love, Lord Jesus, I am confident
that through you I will be delivered from evil,
kept free from sin today,
and protected from all anxiety and worry,
as I wait in joyful hope for your coming.

And I am especially confident, Lord Jesus Christ,
that I will enjoy your peace in my life today,
and peace you promised your apostles when you said:
'I leave you peace, my peace I give you';
the peace that is different from the world's peace;
the peace we have through being united to you;
the peace your apostles passed on
to all who believe the message you entrusted to them.

Prayers before the Blessed Sacrament

Love and mercy (Eucharistic Prayer I, adapted)

I lose your peace when I disobey you by sin.
Forgive my sins, forgive the sins of all your people,
for we have not loved you as we should;
we have been selfish in our response to your love.
We brought sin and suffering to ourselves and others.
But remember your love. Remember your death for us.
Remember the lives and love of your saints
and of all who have given their whole lives to you.
And remember us whom you have chosen.
Remember our faith, the faith of your people;
even though through our weakness we have failed,
remember our efforts and desires, and in your mercy
grant us the peace and unity of your Kingdom
where you live for ever and ever.

Lamb of God, you take away the sins of the world,
have mercy on us.
Lamb of God, you take away the sins of the world,
grant us peace.

Lord Jesus Christ, son of the living God,
by the will of the Father
and the work of the Holy Spirit,
your death brought life to the world.
By your holy body and blood,
free me from all my sins and from every evil.
Keep me faithful to your teaching,
and never let me be parted from you.

Lord Jesus Christ, with faith in your love and mercy,
I desire to eat your body and drink your blood
so that I may have your life in me.
Do not condemn me because of my sinfulness,
but give me lasting health in mind and body.
Lord, I know I am not worthy to receive you,
but only say the word and I shall be healed.

I praise God's love (Eucharistic Prayer 2, adapted)

I come before you with joy, Lord Jesus Christ.
I adore you, Word of God, Second Person of the Trinity.
Through you your Father made the universe,
and sent you as Saviour to redeem his people.

By the power of the Holy Spirit,
you became man and were born of the Virgin Mary.
For my sake you opened your arms on the cross
and accepted a most painful death to save me.
By rising from the dead
you showed that human life does not end at death.

In this, Lord, you fulfilled your Father's will,
and won for him a holy people,
called by baptism to be one with you, our Brother,
as living branches are united to a vine,
as parts of a living body are united to their head,
as wives are united in love with their husbands.

You revealed to us the glorious love of God,
the hidden, eternal, inner life of the Trinity,
which you brought to our world in your human body,
in a particular place and at a particular time.
Living in you, I too share God's life,
as you live in me and share my life.
With you I can enter the hidden life of the Trinity,
living now in the darkness of faith
the life I will enjoy in the clear vision of heaven.

Filled with your love by the power of the Spirit,
I can praise my Father with the angels and saints:
'Holy, holy, holy Lord, God of power and might,
Heaven and earth are full of your glory.
Hosanna in the highest.
Blessed is he who comes in the name of the Lord.
Hosanna in the highest.'

Prayers before the Blessed Sacrament

Sharing Christ's love (Eucharistic Prayer 2, adapted)

I come before you now, Lord Jesus Christ,
because your love made you present on our altar:
Giving thanks to God the night before you died,
you changed bread and wine into your Body and Blood
and you gave your priests the same power
which you commanded them to use in your memory.

So your Mass constantly reminds us of the cross
where your enemies separated your body and blood
and caused your death,
which you offered for our redemption.

So, Lord, when priests use the power you gave them
and put before me the sacramental sign of your death
you enable me to share in your offering on Calvary,
and to offer it to your Father as my own.

Through this sacramental sign of yours,
we proclaim your death, Lord Jesus, until you come.
By your cross and resurrection you set us free.
You are the Saviour of the world.
Dying you destroyed our death;
rising you restored our life;
Lord Jesus, come in glory.

I kneel before your tabernacle, Lord Jesus,
and I renew my faith in the mystery of love,
where your continuing presence reminds me
of the last Mass I offered with you,
and of the union of love
which awaits me when I next receive you.
I thank you for letting me share your sacrifice,
as I renew my offering of your love to the Father,
with all your people called to be united to you.
And when I next receive you in Holy Communion,
I will receive you back from the Father —
the same Gift I offered him at your priest's hands.

For the living and the dead (Eucharistic Prayer 2, adapted)

Help me always to remember that I am never alone.
Each of your people was united to you by Baptism,
and so I am called to be united to them in you,
who came to be Friend and Brother to each of us.
Make us one with one another in love and friendship
so that all people can know we are your followers,
when they see how we love and care for one another.

Help me to grow in your love every day of my life,
together with all your people throughout the world,
especially with the Pope, our bishop, and our priests,
who bring us your sacraments and sacrifice,
and with all who work for the welfare of your people.

Have mercy on my family and friends...
on all who have asked me to pray for them...
on all who are suffering now...
on all your people who are united with you in God...
on those who are separated from you by sin...
on those who do not yet know your Father's love.

Have mercy on my brothers and sisters, Lord Jesus,
who have died trusting in your promise
that they will rise again.
Bring all our dead to heaven
to enjoy for ever with you the hidden life of God
which you share with the Father and the Spirit.

As I kneel before you present in your tabernacle,
I remember that your Saints are also here,
united to you here, as in heaven:
your Virgin Mother Mary, who is our mother also,
your apostles and martyrs and saints,
and all your holy people who have done your will
as they lived in this world of yours in past ages.

As I now know you in the darkness of my faith,
I rejoice that they know you as you really are,
enjoying your friendship as they see you face to face
living with you in the mystery of the Trinity.

Prayers before the Blessed Sacrament

Peace and unity (Eucharistic Prayer 3, adapted)

Jesus, your sacrifice on Calvary, renewed at Mass,
has made our peace with God the Father.
Help your Church now to grow in faith and love.
Strengthen our Pope..., and our Bishop...,
and all the bishops and clergy of your Church,
and all the people you have gained for the Father.
May we continue to bring your peace and salvation
to everyone in the world.

I come before you in hope and love, Lord Jesus.
In your mercy and love, offer to your Father,
the prayers and desires of all your people.
Through their teaching and example and help,
may all God's children, everywhere in this world,
be united in forgiveness and love for one another.

Lord Jesus, take all our dead to heaven,
our brothers and sisters who died in your Church,
and all who left this world in God's friendship.
Through you, my Jesus, I also hope to enjoy
the vision of your Father's glory
sharing the life you enjoy with him and the Spirit
in the inner knowledge and love of the Trinity.

I look forward to my next Communion
when you will again give me the sign of your love,
coming to me under the appearance of bread
so that you will live in me and I will live in you.
Through you, with you and in you, Lord Jesus Christ,
united to your Holy Spirit and inspired by him,
I offer today,
all my life and love to your Father in heaven
to give him glory and honour for ever.

God of love and mercy (Eucharistic Prayer for Reconciliation I, adapted)

Lord Jesus Christ, present in the tabernacle,
you remind me of your Father's love —
that your Father is a God of love and mercy,
always ready to forgive,
asking me to confess and admit that I have sinned,
and to trust in his mercy.

Remaining with us in the Blessed Sacrament,
you are the living proof and sign, Lord Jesus,
that in spite of our many sins,
your Father did not abandon us.

Through you, he bound himself more closely to us,
his human family, his own chosen people,
in a bond that can never be broken,
as he sent you to be born into our human race
born of a woman, a child of Adam.

Lord, like the prodigal son in your parable,
I rise from my sins and return to my Father.
I want to serve him and his family of humankind,
by opening my heart to the fullness of the Spirit.

Lord Jesus, innocent and without sin,
you gave yourself into the hands of human sinners,
into the hands of our brothers who crucified you,
as we could so easily have done had we been there.

But you forgave our sins against you and your people.
Raised up on the cross, you joined earth to heaven,
and you stretched out your hands to embrace humankind,
as you reconciled us with God and with one another.

And you left us a sign of your love for us
in the Mass that renewed your offering on Calvary,
showed us once again your love and forgiveness,
and left you here to remind us always of your love.

Prayers before the Blessed Sacrament

Love and forgiveness (Eucharistic Prayer for Reconciliation 2, adapted)

I believe, Lord Jesus Christ, that through your love
you changed bread and wine into your body and blood,
and remain with us under the appearance of bread
as a constant sign and sacrament of your love,
reminding us of your care for us.

I kneel in your presence, Lord Jesus Christ,
and join you in praising and thanking your Father,
our all-powerful and ever-living God,
for his interest and care for the world he created,
the world he entrusted to the care of his people,
to develop and use it for their welfare
and the welfare of their children,
made in his image and likeness.

But through sin, we are inclined to evil.
Left to ourselves, we selfishly quarrel and fight,
hurting one another in jealousy, hatred, revenge,
refusing to help one another in our needs.

So you came, Lord Jesus, to show us how to love,
to show how important it is to forgive one another
how important it is to reconcile with one another
and to live in friendship and love.

I love and thank you, Lord Jesus, in your tabernacle,
where you are present in the Sacrament of your love,
the Sacrament and Sign of your suffering and death,
which you accepted in love for your Father,
forgiving your enemies and praying for them,
without hatred, bitterness or seeking revenge.

Your presence here, Lord Jesus, is also a sign
that you send your Spirit to change my heart,
leading me to speak to my enemies and serve them,
to make friends with all who hurt me or whom I hurt,
and to seek ways of living in peace with others.

Example of Jesus (Eucharistic Prayer for Reconciliation 2, adapted)

Only through your example, Lord Jesus,
and the work of your Spirit in my soul and my life,
can we end conflict through understanding,
hatred through mercy,
and revenge through forgiveness.
For as you love me, Lord Jesus,
you also love those towards whom I feel bitter.
You died on the cross for them as you died for me.
You call them to heaven, as you call me.
Fill my heart with your love for them.
Help me to see and understand the plan of your Father
that if I refuse to forgive and love them here,
I refuse to live with them in heaven,
and I reject the gift of eternal life you offer me.
For only those who love and serve one another,
in repentance and forgiveness and love for you
can share your life, and live in your love for ever.

You came to us, Lord Jesus Christ,
in the name of the Father,
our God of power and might.
You are the Word bringing salvation from the Father.
You are the Father's hand stretched out to sinners,
the way that leads to his peace,
the truth showing us the value of his people
and the life by which we will share his joy in heaven.

I have often wandered from my Father and his love,
and failed to love those whom he loves,
and whom he sent me to love and serve.
But you have brought me back again and again.
In the plan of the Father, you accepted death
at the hands of your enemies,
so that I might turn again to him,
and find my way to others in love and service,
by understanding and trying to imitate your love,
your love for sinners, of whom I am the greatest.

Prayers before the Blessed Sacrament

Reconciliation (Eucharistic Prayer for Reconciliation 2, adapted)

Kneeling in your presence in your Sacrament of Love,
I recall and celebrate with thanks and joy
the reconciliation you gained us through your death,
in love for your Father
and in love for those who caused your death.

I believe, Lord Jesus,
that you are present in the Blessed Sacrament,
that you came to this church
at a Mass offered with you by your people,
at the hands of your priest,
who changed bread and wine into your body and blood,
recalling your reconciling death on the cross,
and offering it once more to your Father
at a new moment of time.

You are present here as a pledge of your love.
I recall with love your death and resurrection,
and with you, Lord Jesus, I again offer in spirit,
your sacrifice of reconciliation to your Father.

With you, Lord Jesus, our Brother,
we ask your Father to accept us,
who are hurt and divided by sin.
Fill us with your Spirit,
to take away all that divides us.

When I next receive you in Communion, Lord Jesus,
I hope to experience your desire for union with me,
and to enjoy your love for me.
Help me to know you have the same love and desire
for everyone created by your Father,
for everyone you died for,
for those who have hurt me, or whom I have hurt,
and even for those I perhaps consider my 'enemies',
because of some past actions of theirs,
actions perhaps repented of and forgiven by God.

Unity for your Church (Eucharistic Prayer for Reconciliation 2, adapted)

Jesus, in your love we are all united and made one.
May your Spirit keep us in union with one another,
with... our Pope, and... our Bishop,
and with all your priests, and your people everywhere,
but especially with those of this parish.
May your Church, Lord Jesus, everywhere in the world
be a sign of unity and an instrument of your peace,
bringing to all the peace you left to your apostles.

You came to be united to me, Lord Jesus,
as you live in me and I live in you.
May I love and serve those I meet today.
May I never be separated in spirit from anyone
in my mind or heart
through dislike, jealousy, ambition, hatred, pride.

Gather all peoples and countries of the world,
divided by race, language, culture and past hurts,
to be united in peace and harmony in this world,
so all people can give full attention to loving you
with their families and friends,
without the terror, suffering or fear of war.

Unite us all in this life, Lord Jesus,
as we hope to be all united in heaven,
sharing the one eternal banquet of life
to which you invite and call your people,
for whom you gave your life in suffering.

I look forward, Lord Jesus,
to meeting and knowing and loving like you
the millions of people I can never know in this life,
but who will be my friends because they are yours,
not just the few I can know in my human life
but all of them, as I share your life in God,
and know and love them as you do.

The Sacrament of Reconciliation

INTRODUCTION

Whether we call it the Sacrament of Penance, the Sacrament of Reconciliation, or just 'going to confession', the reality of the sacrament Christ left his Church for forgiving sin remains the same. We are grateful for his Sign of Love, which enables us to be certain that our sins are forgiven, and that we can face the future at peace with God and ourselves, and willing to work for the lessening of the 'temporal suffering' our wrong actions or omissions have caused to others.

I hope this section will help those who use it to make more fruitful use of the time they spend preparing for confession and giving thanks afterwards. Those preparing community exercises for the Second Rite of Reconciliation may also find it useful. Above all, I hope that its use will encourage more people to make use of this sacrament for the ongoing personal renewal that we sin-inclined people should make a part of our normal everyday spiritual life.

READINGS FOR CONFESSION

A sign of reconciliation — with God and people

I sin when I disobey laws God gave me for my welfare.
When I sin, I offend God by rejecting him and his love;
I hurt myself, by doing something that is bad for me;
I hurt others also, many of whom I will never know here.
In repentance, I turn back to God, who forgives me my sin;
I accept my own hurt as just punishment for my sins;
I pray that others will forgive me, as God forgives me.

Christ gave priests the power to forgive sin in his name.
They use this in the sacrament of reconciliation, penance.
When I repent, God can truly forgive without the sacrament.
Penance is the sign of my repentance and God's forgiveness.
It is also an effective sign of my reparation and penance.
In it I humble myself by confessing to my priest-brother
and I accept and carry out the 'penance' he gives me.

When I hurt a friend, I need to apologize and be forgiven.
I cannot apologize personally to all I have hurt by sin.
The Sacrament of Penance helps me to fulfill this need.
It is the sign of my reconciliation with my fellow-sinners.

In confessing to his priest, I apologize to God who sees me.
In doing so I apologize also to all the people I have hurt,
for the priest is their representative as well as God's.
His absolution is the sign that they forgive as God does,
for he speaks in the name of all members of the Church.
Through them, he speaks in the name of all the world.
His absolution is the sign that I am again a friend to all.

Jesus is the Son of his Father, and brother to us all.
In absolution he forgives in the name of God, his Father,
and also forgives us in the name of our family members.

Penance is the sign of reconciliation with all we know.
We can make it real by forgiving all from our heart.

Vices, temptation and sin

As a result of original sin, we are all inclined to evil.
We find the vices easier to follow than the virtues.
The vices or 'capital sins', are listed under headings:
pride, covetousness, lust, anger, gluttony, envy, sloth.
These are not really 'sins', until we give in to them.
If we always do what we want to do, we soon do wrong.
An act rejecting a vice or temptation is good and holy.
Thus we should recognize a vice as soon as it affects us.
Vices affect everybody but they are not always recognized.
One who does not know a vice is not thereby free of it,
but may be giving in to it without even knowing it is bad.

Vice is a big source of temptation, but not the only one.
The devil and the bad example of others also tempt us.
Three rules help me to reject temptation of thought:
a) I say a short prayer to God or to my patron saint;
b) I bring something else deliberately into my mind;
c) I change what I am doing — at least my bodily position.

When we reject temptation, we strengthen good habits,
which make it easier for us to do good in the future.
In our lives, we usually experience vice before virtue.
In knowing and rejecting vice, I will experience virtue.
As I examine my life to see the sins I have committed,
I should also try to see what vices led me to each sin.
I should try to learn not merely how I sinned, but why.

To weaken vice should not be the ultimate end of my life.
Neither should I seek virtue merely for its own sake.
My main aim should always be to love God and others.
Virtues help me do this, and vices hinder me.
I strengthen virtue and weaken vice for one reason only —
to enable me to love God and others more easily.

Confession

I should confess all serious sins not already confessed.
My confession is bad if I knowingly conceal such a sin;
it is not bad if I forget a sin, or make an honest mistake;
the sin is forgiven, but I should confess it the next time.
To prepare well, I try to recall how I broke God's law.
I examine my actions in the light of God's commandments.
I also try to see the reasons and motives for my sin:
pride? covetousness? lust? anger? gluttony? envy? sloth?
How have I loved God — prayer? faith? obedience? Mass?
How have I served or hurt the people to whom I am sent:
Husband/wife? children? parents? family? neighbours?
employees? employer? fellow-workers? enemies?
strangers?

Contrition

Confession is useless without true sorrow or repentance.
When sorrow is true, God forgives even outside confession.
When preparing for confession, I tell God that I repent:
'O God, be merciful to me a sinner.'
'Lord, remember me when you come into your kingdom.'
'Father, I have sinned; treat me as your hired servant.'
I recall God's love which I rejected when I sinned.
I remember Christ's sufferings on Calvary for my sins.
I recall the punishment my unrepented sins deserve.
If at death I totally reject God, I do so for all eternity.
To know God's law is a privilege only some enjoy.
Unlike so many others, I know God's law and his love.
So people around me have a right to expect my help.
When I sin I refuse them that help, and I hurt them.
My repentance will include a complete turning from sin.
I resolve not to sin again, though I know my weakness.
But I am weak, so I ask God to help me keep my
    resolution.
I try to foresee what leads to sin, so that I may avoid it.
I pray the 'acts of contrition' that best express my sorrow.

Absolution

A good preparation includes real repentance and sorrow
through which God can forgive us even before absolution.
But Christ commands us to submit our sins to the Church,
by confessing our sins to a priest to receive absolution.
Absolution is the priest's statement that we are forgiven.
It is the public seal and guarantee that we are forgiven.
It is like a receipt that shows a debt has been paid.
Through it, Christ forgives any sins not already forgiven.
While on earth, he proved he had power to forgive sin.
Now he uses priests to exercise that same power:
He said: 'If you forgive people's sins, they are forgiven.'
The confessor is bound strictly by the 'seal of confession'.
He is strictly forbidden to reveal what was confessed.
He may not use it, or even show that he knows it.
In repentance, before confession, we hope God forgives us.
After absolution, we know by faith that he has forgiven us.

Satisfaction

The 'penance' priests give is also sometimes called
    'satisfaction'.
Nothing we human people do can fully satisfy for our sins.
Sin offends God, our infinite Creator and loving Father.
Unrepented and unforgiven sin deserves hell or purgatory.
Only Jesus, the God-Man could fully satisfy for our sins.
The 'satisfaction' he offered was his death on the cross.
Because this death satisfied for our sin, God forgives us.
God reveals his commandments to us for our welfare.
In them he shows us the best way to live in this world.
When we reject his way, human suffering increases,
for ourselves and others, here in this world of time.
We can undo and lessen this 'temporal punishment',
by helping others to a better and happier and holier life,
by forgiving and praying for others, as Jesus himself did.
Our 'penance' is a sign that we will work for this,
and that we accept whatever suffering God sends us,
as a fair share of the human suffering we have added to.

Right living   (based on Ephesians 4)

Don't live like heathens whose minds are dark.
Get rid of your old self, by which you lived badly.
Put on the new self, created in God's likeness.
No more lying! Everyone must tell the truth.
Stop stealing, and start working to help the poor.
Use words that will do good to those who meet you.
Never hurt others in what you say.
Get rid of all bitterness, passion and anger.
No more shouting, insults or any hateful feelings.
Be kind and tender-hearted to one another.
Forgive one another, as God has forgiven you.
Do not even speak of sexual immorality or indecency,
or greed, which makes a god out of money.
Do not use obscene, profane or vulgar language.
No one that is immoral, indecent or greedy
will share the kingdom of Christ and God.
Do not let anyone deceive you with foolish words.
You are the Lord's people — learn what pleases him.
Do not get drunk.
Praise God from your heart in prayer and song.
Submit yourselves to one another because of Christ.
Wives, submit to your husbands as to the Lord.
Husbands, love your wives as Jesus loved the Church.
Children, respect and obey parents as a duty to God.
Parents, do not make your children angry.
Train them with Christian teaching and discipline.
Never steal; obey employers with a sincere heart
because of your reverence to the Lord.
Whatever you do, work at it with all your heart.
Employers, treat your workers justly and fairly,
in heaven you have the same Master as them.
Persevere in prayer and keep awake as you pray.
Let your speech be always pleasing and interesting.

Holiness and sin
(based on 2 Tim 3, 1 Thess. 4:3, Heb. 13, James 3)

Keep away from sinners and do not imitate them:
those who are selfish, greedy, boastful, conceited,
insulting, disobedient, ungrateful, irreligious,
unkind, merciless, slanderers, violent, fierce,
treacherous, reckless, and swollen with pride,
hating good, and loving pleasure rather than God.
Christian in name, but rejecting Christ's power,
deceiving others and being deceived themselves,
refusing to listen to sound and true teaching,
following their own sinful desires,
and teachers who tell them what they want to hear.

Instead, welcome strangers into your home.
Worship God in a way that will please him.
Help those in prison and those who suffer.
Keep your minds free from love of money.
Obey your leaders and respect the church ministers,
who guide and instruct you in Christian living,
for they must account to God for their service.

Be holy and completely free from sexual immorality.
Husbands and wives must be faithful to each other;
and live together in a holy and honourable way,
not with lustful desire as the heathens do.
Do not wrong your fellow-Christian, or cheat him.
Live quietly, mind your business, earn your living.
Warn the idle, encourage the timid, help the weak.
Be patient with all. Never pay back wrong for wrong.
Do good to one another — and to all those you meet.
Be joyful always, and always pray and be thankful.
Be quick to listen, slow to speak, slow to anger.
Get rid of filthy habits and wicked conduct.
Control your tongue or your religion is worthless.
Do not be jealous, bitter or selfish in your heart.
Desires for pleasure cause quarrels and fighting.
If you strongly desire things you cannot get,
you are ready to quarrel and fight and even to kill.

PRAYERS BEFORE CONFESSION

The soul's offering (M.W. Brew)

I come to you, my Lord,
with tearful eyes and bruised and bleeding feet,
torn by the world's hard ways and stony streets,
its deserts bleak and bare;
sore, wounded, and in bitter misery,
and heavy laden, save alone to you
can I go anywhere?
Whene'er I turn from you, I lose the light
that guided me before through darkest night,
and blindly feel my way
on the hard road of sinfulness and wrong,
stumbling and falling as I go along
with hope all taken away.
O lead me, Lord, unto your feet anew,
the feet that once for me
were tired and bleeding too.

Prayers before Confession

I come to you, O Lord,
an idle servant and with empty hands,
the prodigal from distant foreign lands,
where all my store was spent.
Nothing have I to say, but silent wait
before the pillars of your mercy-gate.
With drooping head and bent,
until the time when you will travel by
and seeing all my weakness, cast your eye
on one so worn and weak,
one who has not the wedding garment on
and lost the light that once upon him shone,
and who can nothing speak,
save that one cry that always heard will be,
'I am a sinner, Lord,
be merciful to me.'

I come to you, my Lord,
and yet I have no gift that I can bring,
such as may give you joy, O thorn-crowned king;
none save myself alone,
and my tired heart that wandered sinfully,
seeking for joys upon the world's wild sea,
for peace, yet finding none.
Will you accept this worthless offering?
Alas! dear Lord, 'tis all I have to bring —
how poor and yet my all!
And, knowing this, you will not turn away
but bend your ear to listen while I pray,
and on your name I call.
Gather up once more life's broken strands,
and bless your child once more
with your dear wounded hands.

Acts of repentance (based on scripture)

If I say I have no sin, I deceive myself,
and the truth is not in me.
O heavenly Father, if I confess my sins,
you are faithful and just to forgive me,
and to cleanse me from all my evil-doing.
You do not desire the death of the wicked,
but that I turn from my sinful ways and live.

O God, my Father, I have sinned against you.
I have done what is evil in your sight.
I am not worthy to be called your son.

O Lord, be merciful to me, a sinner.
Have mercy on me because of your greatness;
and because of your love, forgive my sins,
as I forgive those who sin against me.
I have sinned,
and I have not received what I deserved.

For you, O God, are merciful and gracious,
patient, and full of love, and true.
You know all things;
even though I have sinned in the past,
you know that I love you.
What have I in heaven but you and your love?
Besides you, what do I desire upon earth?
What good did I have from those sins
of which I am now ashamed?
You are the God of my heart
and the God who is my choice for ever.

I will turn away from sin and do good.
Lead me not into temptation, deliver me from evil.
I will always keep your law,
because it is yours, and you are my God.

Sin and mercy (based on Romans 1)

God, help me to understand what you have revealed,
that you punish sin, which keeps us from knowing you.

When I offend you, Lord, I deserve to be punished,
for I know from the beauty of what you have made,
that you are my powerful Creator and my infinite God;
and so I have no excuse when I sin.
When I sin, I worship and serve created things,
instead of worshipping and serving you who made them
and I refuse you the honour and thanks I owe you,
as the first need of my existence and my life.

So, because I have exchanged your truth for a lie
my sins provide their own punishments,
They darken my mind so I do not judge correctly
and I am given over completely to shameful passions.
And I am led in turn to further sins,
and I multiply the punishments I deserve,
through impurity, jealousy, greed and hatred,
through treachery, deceit, spite and lies,
through backbiting and gossip,
through neglecting God, and turning away from him,
through insolence, arrogance, boastfulness, pride,
through refusing love and mercy to those who need it,
through disobedience to parents,
and unfaithfulness to promises.
Help me to see these sins creeping into my life.
Help me to set my mind against them,
and never to encourage them in myself or in others.

When I sin, Lord, you are patient and kind to me,
because you want to draw me to repentance.
Help me not to abuse your love by refusing to repent,
or by using it as an excuse for not repenting.
Have mercy on me, Lord, have mercy on me.
Do not punish me as I deserve.

Sinful desires (based on Romans 6,7)

Lord, I have offended you. Have mercy on me.
I have allowed myself to be ruled by my sinfulness,
and given my body to sin.

Help me, O Lord, to refuse to give myself to sin,
to refuse to use any power of my life for evil.
I surrender myself completely to you,
that I may do your will, and carry out your plan.
Give me strength to be no longer a slave of sin,
but to choose freely to serve and follow you.
Let me obey you, Lord, and not my sinful desires,
for you have given me your truth and your love,
to set me free from the slavery of sin.
Make me your slave forever, to carry out your will.

I have been a slave to sin, have mercy on me.
I have rejected goodness, have mercy on me.
I am ashamed of what I have done, have mercy on me.
I have deserved punishment, have mercy on me.
I have hurt myself and others, have mercy on me.
Give me a life completely dedicated to you.
Help me to live in union with Christ Jesus my Lord,
sharing your divine life through him in baptism.

I hate my sins. I reject them.
I promise to reject them in the future.
But I know my weakness.
I know your love, and want to serve and obey you —
but my sinful desires are strong, and drag me down.
I find a different power in my body,
a power that fights in me against your law of love,
a power so strong it can overpower and enslave me,
so strong that alone I cannot resist it.
But I know I am not alone. I know you are with me.
I know that Jesus your Son, by his love and power,
will rescue me from the desires that enslave me.

Prayers before Confession

Devotion to God (St Augustine)

O Lord Jesus, let me know myself, let me know you,
and desire nothing else but only you.

Let me hate myself and love you,
and do all things for the sake of you.

Let me humble myself and exalt you,
and think of nothing but only you.

Let me die to myself and live in you,
and take whatever happens as coming from you.

Let me forget myself, and walk after you,
and ever desire to follow you.

Let me flee from myself and turn to you,
that so I may merit to be defended by you.

Let me fear for myself, let me fear you,
and be amongst those who are chosen by you.

Let me distrust myself and trust in you
and always pray for the love of you.

Let me cling to nothing but only you.
Look upon me that I may love you.

Call me that I may see you
and forever possess you.

Jerome's prayer for mercy

Show me your mercy, Lord. Delight my heart with it.
Let me find you, whom I seek with great longing.
Behold! I am like the man whom the robbers seized,
and beat, and left half-dead on the road to Jericho.
Jesus Christ, kind-hearted Samaritan, come to my aid!

I am the lost sheep, wandering in the desert.
Seek after me, O good Shepherd,
bring me home to your fold.
Do with me according to your will,
so that I may live with you all the days of my life,
and praise you for all eternity
with all those who are with you in heaven.

I live with Christ (based on Romans 8)

You taught us, Lord, and we know from experience,
that the natural effect of sin,
is to lead to suffering and death.
But by the death of Christ
and the action of his Spirit,
you freed us from this law and the effects of sin.
You sent your Son, Jesus Christ, truly a man,
like us in everything except sin,
to bear in himself the sufferings our sins deserve,
and free us from the law combining sin and death,
by fulfilling it in his death for the sins of others.

As long therefore as I live in union with Christ,
I have no fear of being condemned or punished.
But if I live as my human nature wants me to live,
my mind is soon controlled by my sinful desires;
I cannot take advantage of Christ's death,
and I will merit the punishment of death for myself.

If I live by the Spirit, and am led by the Spirit,
I kill my sinful actions, and I live as your child.
For your Spirit makes me your child,
and gives me the power to call you 'Father'.
Thus, I will possess the blessings
which you, my Father, have prepared for me,
as I share them with Christ, your divine Son,
and with all others whom you have chosen.

Even if I share his sufferings here,
I will more surely share his glory in heaven.
I know your power and your love for me,
I believe that you created me for happiness,
and every day of my life, I believe and confess
that whatever I suffer in this life
cannot be compared with the glory prepared for me.
Help me each day to live in the hope of this faith,
until you come to show me the truth of what I hope.

Prayers before Confession

Lord, have mercy (based on 1 John 1 and 2)

You are Light eternal,
and there is no darkness in you.
You give us your light and your love through Christ,
to enable us avoid the darkness of ignorance and sin.

I left your way, Lord.
I lost your light and your love.
I was yours no longer; no longer was I united to you.
But the blood of Jesus cleansed all my sins,
and enabled me once more to walk in your light.

I need Jesus Christ and his power of forgiveness.
If I refuse to admit that I have sinned,
I am a liar, and the truth is not in me.
I admit that I have sinned, Lord.
Through your priest, I confess to you and your Church.
Have mercy on me, Lord, and forgive me,
and make me clean from all my wrongdoing,
through the death of Christ, who intercedes for me.

I will really know that I love you,
only by obeying your commandments.
If I pray: 'I believe in you' or 'I love you',
while refusing to know or obey your commandments,
I am a liar and the truth is not in me.
Help me to live as Jesus Christ lived,
obeying your will, and fulfilling your plan,
so that I may know I am living in you and with you.
Help me not to love what is sinful in the world.
Help me to refuse and reject all temptation, Lord,
even though it is what my sinful nature desires,
or what my greed and avarice urge me to do,
or what many people in the world put great value on.
These come from what is sinful in the world.
But the world and everything in it is passing away,
but you never pass away, Lord, you will live for ever.
And living as you want me to live,
I also can live for ever with you in Jesus Christ.

Prayer for pardon (adapted from St Augustine)

Before your eyes, O Lord, we bring our sins,
and compare them
with the punishment we have received.
If we examine the evil of our sins,
what we suffer is little, what we deserve is great;
what we committed is exceedingly offensive,
what we have suffered is very slight.

We see how our sin hurts others,
and we feel some of its resulting suffering ourselves
which is your in-built punishment for our wrong-doing;
yet we are still stubborn in sinning.
You chastise us for our unfaithfulness,
yet our sinfulness is not changed.
Our suffering soul is afflicted,
but we are too proud to bow to your justice.
We groan under the sorrows of our life,
yet we make no real effort to improve.

If you spare us, we return to our sinful ways;
If you punish us, we cannot endure it.
When you correct us through trials,
we confess our wrongdoing;
but after your correction,
we forget that we have wept.

If you stretch out your hand, we promise to amend:
if you withhold your sword, we forget our promise.
If you strike, we cry out for mercy.
If you spare, we soon provoke you to strike again.
We come before you, Lord, confessing we are guilty.
We know that unless you pardon us,
we shall deserve to perish.
Almighty Father, grant, without our deserving it,
that pardon we ask,
for you made us out of nothing.

PRAYERS AFTER CONFESSION

Our hope in Christ (based on Romans 5)

Turning to you in faith, O God, our Father,
we have been put right with you and made holy,
and we have peace with you through Jesus our Lord.
He has brought us, through loving faith
into the grace of God in which we now live.
And so we rejoice
in the hope we have of sharing your glory.

We rejoice even when we are troubled,
for we know that trouble leads to patience
patience brings perseverance,
and perseverance strengthens hope.
This hope does not disappoint us,
for you have poured out your love into our hearts
by the Holy Spirit, your Gift to us.

For while mankind was still helpless in wickedness
Christ died for us,
when the time chosen by you had come.
You have shown us how much you love us,
for we were still sinners, when Christ died for us.

By his death, mankind was put right with you,
and so we hope that each one of us
will be saved from your wrath and punishment.
We were your enemies, but you made us your friends
through the death of your Son.
And because we are your friends,
we are confident that we will be saved
by Jesus, your Son, living with us and in us.

We rejoice in you, through our Lord Jesus Christ,
because he has made us friends of yours
to share with him your life and love.

To amend my life (based on Romans 2)

If we sin, Lord, and refuse to repent,
you have warned us that we will be punished.
But if we do good, and give glory to you
you will reward us with peace, happiness and glory.

We know what you want us to do.
We have learned from your teaching
how to choose what is right.
We are certain that, in this teaching you gave us,
we know all the truth we need for living.
So we need not waste time seeking elsewhere for more,
but can give all our mind and heart to loving you,
in the daily circumstances and situations we meet.

You chose us and sent us to those around us.
You gave us your law to help them more effectively.
You want us to guide those who are blind,
to enlighten those who are in darkness,
to instruct the ignorant, and to teach the young.

We cannot do this effectively
unless we practise what we teach.
Help us never to bring shame on you,
by refusing to obey your law,
while we proclaim and teach it to others.

In your kindness, Lord, you lead me to repent.
Soften my hard and stubborn heart for the future,
for in my selfishness I often reject what is good,
and run the risk of your anger and punishment.

Help me repent, Lord, and to be ready for the day
when your Son, Jesus Christ, will come to me,
to judge my secret thoughts and make them known.
Help me to obey your law every day
and to turn back to you in sorrow whenever I sin,
and so fulfill my destiny and live forever with you.

Prayers after Confession

Free to serve others (based on Galatians 5)

Lord, you called us to be free to serve others;
and in this freedom I will find my true happiness.
Do not let me use a false idea of 'freedom',
as an excuse for 'doing what I like',
or for letting my sinful desires rule over me.
Your freedom, Lord, is freedom to love and serve,
a freedom from passion and from the power of Satan,
a freedom from selfishness and from all my vices.

To love my neighbour, Lord, in your freedom,
I must obey all your commandments.
If I make no effort to love my neighbour,
if I refuse to serve or help him when I can,
my selfish instincts will gain control of my acts
and I will become like a wild animal
attacking and being attacked, hurting and being hurt,
until I destroy myself and my friends.
I love and respect myself, Lord, because you love me,
and you chose me as a unique and individual person.
I can give you a love that no one else can give;
you love me, and so you chose me and created me.
Help me to love and respect others as myself, Lord,
for you love them and chose them, as you did me.
They exist; and so, as I believe that you love me,
with that same faith, I believe that you love them,
and chose each as a different and unique person
for existence and for life and for love.

May I never be proud or jealous, or anger others,
May I never be angry, ambitious, envious, hateful.
May I never turn against others, or hurt them.
I belong to you, Lord and die to these desires.
May the Spirit who brings me your life, control me
so that I may live in love, joy, patience, kindness,
goodness, faithfulness, humility and self-control.

Remaining faithful (based on James 1)

In time of temptation, Lord God my Father,
help me to remain faithful to you,
so that I may receive the reward of happiness
which you have promised to those who love you.

When I give in to temptation, I give birth to sin,
and sin in turn gives birth to suffering and death.
When I pray for the help you are always ready to give,
and you help me to overcome and reject temptation,
I show the value of my faith, and I prove my love,
and I strengthen myself against future temptations.
Thus, I am confident that I can persevere,
working with courage for the joy you promise,
and seeking for nothing that you cannot give me.
Lord, I hope in you; I trust in your love for me.
Remove my doubts, lest I be tossed about,
as a wave of the sea is tossed about by the wind.

Help me to avoid sin, and to weaken my bad habits,
so that I may submit myself gladly to you,
and receive and welcome your word into my heart.
Help me see my selfishness in the mirror of your love
and my sinfulness in the mirror of your holiness.
Help me to keep looking at you, and praying to you,
until I am forced to change and become like you.
Help me to know your law, which frees me for love.
Help me to love it and put it into practice,
so that I may be blessed in all that I do.

Help me always be ready to listen, slow to speak,
and slow also to take offence and become angry;
for your cause and plan is never helped by anger.
Help me to control what I say in conversation, Lord,
to be kind to widows and orphans who need my help,
and to refuse to follow
the bad example I see around me in this world.

False teachers (based on 2 Peter 2)

Lord, help me against false teachers of today.
I will recognise their opinions as untrue
when they reject you and your teaching, Lord Jesus.
Help me not to follow their sinful ways,
into sins of lust and contempt for your Church.

Their love for sin is never satisfied,
and so they try to lead us astray.
They sin in public to make us less ashamed of sin,
and sneer at holiness which they have never experienced.
They tell us that lust and greed are good,
enticing us by the desires of our sinful instincts,
by our darkness of mind and our weakness of will,
using fine-sounding words without truth or meaning
to trap us into believing in them
rather than in you and your Church.

Help me, Lord, to realize they have gone astray.
They have left the straight road of your love,
and are under your curse and punishment.
They cannot bring others the joy of your freedom,
because in leading others to destructive habits,
they have themselves become slaves of these habits,
as people are slaves of whatever overcomes them.

Lord Jesus Christ, help me choose your way.
You do not want anyone to be destroyed.
Help me to turn from my sins and live.
Help me to wait for your coming,
and to remain innocent and good in your sight,
and to enjoy the peace you came to bring me.
Help me to know and love you each day of my life.
Lord Jesus, I choose you as my leader and guide.
To you be glory and honour now and forever.

Love others (based on 1 John 3)

I confess I have sinned Lord, by disobeying you.
I thank you for sending Jesus, himself without sin
to forgive me and show me how to live without sin.
He gave himself fully to love you and his fellow men.
In all his actions, he perfectly fulfilled your plan.
Help me to love without sin, by living as he did,
by living in him, and by him, and united to him.

If I am united to Jesus, you are truly my Father,
and I am your child, sharing your nature and life.
I cannot remain your child if I continue to sin,
and especially if I do not love and serve my brothers.
This is the message we heard from the beginning:
we will know that we are really your children
if we love one another.
Cain failed this test when he killed his brother
and anyone who commits any sin, anywhere, any time,
in some way hurts some brother or sister of his,
somewhere, in some way, then or in the future.

Help me to realize that in each action of my life
I have a choice, Lord, between you and the devil,
between your way of life and his way of life.
Help me to choose you in each action of my life.
Strengthen me, for I can expect the world to hate me,
I will be called foolish by the wise of this world;
People who choose differently will laugh at me.
Christ showed his love for us by dying for us.
Help us be ready to die for him and for one another;
or at least be ready to bear opposition for his sake.

Help me, Lord, to be active in my love for others,
loving them not merely in fine but empty words,
but showing the truth of my love in deed and action.
For if I see my brother in need anywhere in the world,
and refuse him any help I am able to give him,
I cannot be your friend, or a follower of your Son.

St Gertrude's Resolution

O almighty and most merciful God,
according to your most tender mercy,
you have received me back once more.
I have gone astray from you so many times.

I thank you with all the strength of my soul
for this and for all other graces and blessings
you have given me.
I throw myself down at your sacred feet,
and I offer myself to be yours for ever more.

Let nothing in life or death
ever separate me from you.
I am sorry for all the sins of my past life.
I promise again what was promised in my baptism.
From this moment,
I give myself wholly to your love and service.
Grant that for the time to come
I may hate sin more than death itself,
and avoid all such occasions and company
as have led me unhappily into sin.

The Sacrament of Marriage

People give one another the Sacrament when they marry. They live it with one another each day of their lives. The prayers below show the ideals they should aim at, in concepts drawn from scripture and church writings.

PRAYERS FOR MARRIED COUPLES

Married love   (based on the Marriage Rite, Blessings 1,3)

In the beginning you created the universe
and made mankind in your own likeness.
You gave man the constant help of woman,
so that in marriage, they should become one flesh,
and that what you have united, may never be divided.

Father, our union as man and wife is a holy mystery,
for it symbolizes the love of Christ and his Church.

Father, keep us always true to your commandments.
Keep us faithful in marriage,
and let us be living examples of Christian life.
Give us the strength which comes from the gospel,
so that we may be witnesses of Christ to others.

Lord, may we both praise you when we are happy,
and turn to you in our sorrows.
May we be glad that you help us in our work
and know that you are with us in all our needs.

Bless us with children, and help us to be good parents.
May we live to see our children's children,
and after a happy old age,
grant us the fullness of life with the saints,
in the happiness of heaven.

Prayers for Married Couples

For husband and wife (based on the Marriage Rite, Blessing 2)

Father, we are people you created in your image.
You made us a man and a woman,
to be joined as husband and wife
in union of heart and body in marriage
and so fulfil our mission in this world.

Father, you planned to reveal your love,
by making our union as husband and wife
an image, a sign, a sacrament,
of the covenant between you and your people.
As we live out our sacrament in daily life,
our marriage will become a sign
of the marriage between Christ and the Church,
and our love will become a sign of that love.

Father, stretch out your hand over us today,
and bless us in our married life.
Grant, that as we live this sacrament,
we may share with each other the gift of your love,
and become one in heart and mind,
witnessing your presence in our marriage.
Help us to create a home together.
Give us children to be formed by your Good News,
and to have a place in your family.

(Give your blessing to me, your daughter,
so that I may be a good wife and mother,
faithful in love for my family,
generous and kind in caring for our home.)

(Give your blessing to me, your son,
so that I may be a faithful husband and good father.)

Father, as we gather around your table on earth,
grant us one day to enter your feast in heaven,
sharing in the joy of Christ our Lord,
with you and the Holy Spirit for ever.

Wife's Prayer (based on Ephesians 5)

O Lord Jesus Christ, I accept as head of our family,
the husband I chose,
because this is your plan,
and you also chose him for me.

Help me to obey him as saints have obeyed you,
in a spirit of love, not in a spirit of fear,
in a desire to please him and not to please myself.

I can never love as your Church loves you,
for through your presence she is holy,
without spot or wrinkle or imperfection.

But I believe that in the sacrament of our marriage,
I can get help from my union with my husband,
just as your Church gets help and strength
through her union with you.

Prayers for Married Couples

Husband's prayer (based on Ephesians 5)

O Lord Jesus Christ,
I want to love the wife your love has given me.
I want to love her with the same kind of love
that you showed when you died for me.
Though I am weak, and often selfish and uncaring,
help me to love my wife in such a way
that her happiness becomes my happiness,
and I find my joy in giving her joy,
caring for her body as I care for my own.

Grant that the decisions we must sometimes make
in order to keep us together according to your will,
may always be based on our love for each other
and on my desire for her happiness.

Through your sacrament of marriage,
may your love always feed me and care for me,
and strengthen me against my selfishness.

Prayer of Tobias

We praise you, Lord, God of our fathers,
and praise your name for ever and ever.
Let the heavens bless you,
and all the things you have made,
for evermore.
O Lord our God, you created Adam,
and you created Eve as his wife
to help and support him,
and from these two the human race was born.

It was you who said
'It is not good that the man should be alone;
let us make him a helpmate like himself.'
And so, we do not take one another
for any lustful motives, but in singleness of heart.
Be kind enough to have pity on us,
and bring us to old age together.

We praise you, O Lord God,
with every prayer and blessing that is pure;
may you be blessed and praised for evermore.

You are blessed for having made us glad.
What we feared has not happened.
You have treated us with mercy beyond all measure.

You are blessed for taking pity on us,
your son and your daughter.
Grant us, Master, your grace and your protection,
to live out our lives in happiness and grace.

Love and marriage (based on *Humanae Vitae*)

Human life is such a wonderful gift, Lord
that giving it to others is the most serious duty
you have entrusted to us married couples.
We thank you for calling us to share in this privilege,
with its joys and its difficulties,
its happiness and its sorrow.

To understand married love,
we must have faith in you and your plan.
Help us remember your plan for your people:
that we are called not merely to a life in this world,
but also to a supernatural and never-ending life
in the joys of heaven with you.
Marriage itself was created by you, Lord,
and marriage-love comes from you,
who are love itself, calling yourself our 'Father',
from whom every family in heaven and earth is named.

Father, when you chose each of us for life,
you created a separate person,
with a 'self' that belongs to each person alone.
In our married love,
we freely give our 'selves' to one another,
drawn together into a fully satisfying union,
co-operating with you to bring children to life,
and showing them how to live here and for heaven.

Our love shows the union of Christ and the Church,
and Christ has made our marriage a sacrament,
to bring us grace and help in our needs.
Let our love for one another be fully human,
belonging to body and soul at the same time,
a deliberate act of our free will and choice,
as well as a feeling of mutual and joy-giving love.
We pray that it may live and grow
through the joys and sorrows of daily life
as we love God and our neighbour together,
with one heart, one soul, one mind and one strength.

Responsible parenthood (based on *Humanae Vitae*)

Help us, Lord, to be responsible parents,
knowing and respecting the way you made our bodies,
and the laws of passing on life,
which form part of our nature as human persons.

Help us, Lord, to be responsible parents
controlling our bodily desires and passions,
through our reason and will.

Help us, Lord, to be responsible parents
generously deciding to raise a large family,
or deciding to avoid a new birth for a time,
for important reasons, and respecting your law.

Let us always respect the plan you showed
when you created us as man and woman,
able to understand and control
the male and female bodily powers
you created for use in marriage.
Every marriage act is not followed by a new life,
for you have wisely built into our natures, Lord,
natural periods of fertility and infertility
which of themselves and in your plan,
cause a separation in the succession of births.
So, when an act of love is unfruitful in your plan,
it remains lawful and good and holy,
for it expresses our love as husband and wife.

We accept your plan, Lord, that each marriage act,
should remain open to passing on human life,
because you planned one and the same marriage act,
to enable us to express and increase our love,
and to enable us to conceive children.

Help us to understand and accept
that this connection is willed by you,
and may not be broken by us.

Love and children (based on *Humanae Vitae*)

Lord, help our love to be unselfish and complete,
as we share everything generously with one another,
without keeping anything back,
without measuring how much we are going to give;
each of us loving for the sake of the other,
each glad to make the other happy by giving oneself.

Lord, keep us faithful in our love until death.
Help us to refuse our married love to everyone else
as we promised on the day we married.
This is needed for the happiness of our marriage,
and indeed for its very existence.

Grant that we may be fruitful in our love, Lord,
not confining it to ourselves alone,
but embracing into the circle of our family love,
the new lives that will be created through our love.

For you placed this law in the bodies you gave us,
that the act of marital union
that unites us in love as husband and wife
is the same act that enables us to generate life.
Help us never to use this action without love
for you intended it to express our union and love.
And because you intended it also to pass on life,
help us respect this responsibility as we use it.

Help us, Lord, to use our gift of married love well
and to respect the laws of its life-giving powers.
Let us co-operate with your plan, our creating God,
or we do not ourselves control the source of life,
nor do we have unlimited right over our power of sex
which of its structure is intended for new life.
And human life is sacred, Lord,
for your creating hand is present from its beginning,
in your choice of each new person you create.

Loving God in one another

O God, you created us in your image and likeness,
able to know and love you,
able to know and love one another,
able to know and love you in one another
as we see your image and likeness in one another,
and in our children.

You created us male and female, Lord,
so that in our love for one another,
we could share in your creation
by passing on human life.

You made us as particular individual unique persons,
each different from every other person in the world.
So, our love for one another is also unique,
and together we can give you
the love and service that you want from us,
and that no other couple in the world can give.

Make our marriage fruitful, Lord,
in love and service of one another,
in love and service of the world as your family,
and in children who will honour and love you,
children whom you have created through our love
and who would not have existed except for us
and our part in your plan.

We have left our fathers and mothers
so as to give ourselves to one another,
and become one flesh for life in a Christian family
where our love results in children
whom we will rear and teach and train,
to increase the love of our family,
and its service to the people of the world.

Devotion to our Lady

INTRODUCTION

Mary of Nazareth was, and is, a human person. So what is said about the saints in the next section of this book applies to her also. However, because of her special place in our love and devotion, she is given a special place in this book also.

We honour Mary in a special way and more than the other saints, because her Son, Jesus Christ, is God the Son, who took flesh in her womb by the power of the Holy Spirit, and received from her the human life that made him a member of our race, the human heart that loved us and the mouth that taught us, the hands and feet that were nailed to the cross. Because he had no earthly or human father, his whole human being and nature came from Mary, and he must have looked very like her and her family.

PRAYING THE MYSTERIES OF THE ROSARY

HOW TO PRAY THE ROSARY

Praying the rosary well

The rosary has been the most effective prayer for millions of Catholics for many centuries. It has led those who prayed it well to close union with God in their daily lives.

The fifteen traditional mysteries record important events in God's saving plan for his people. We hope that these pages will help people to meditate on each of these events while using the words of the Hail Mary.

The Hail Mary is a biblical prayer

We should value the Hail Mary as one of the most biblical of all traditional prayers.

When we use it, we praise Mary in words first addressed to her by God himself. The angel Gabriel was *sent from God* to say to her, 'Hail, full of grace, the Lord is with you!' (Luke 1:26-28). Elizabeth was *filled with the Holy Spirit* when she praised Mary with the words, 'Blessed are you among women, and blessed is the fruit of your womb' (Luke 1:41-42). And in using these words to praise Mary, we are fulfilling the biblical prophecy she herself made: 'Henceforth, all generations will call me "blessed"' (Luke 1:48).

Response — Holy Mary

In our personal prayer it is sometimes useful for us to say the three words, 'us, sinners, now' slowly, meditating on what they could mean for us. Thus we could pray:

Holy Mary, Mother of God, pray for:

Us Not just for me, but for all your children, in the church and outside it, those who love you and those who do not even know you, all of whom, as individuals or groups, I can include with myself in the word 'us'.

Us sinners Just as I do not pray for myself alone, so I do not pray for 'sinners', without including myself, because I also need mercy and forgiveness.

Us sinners now We need help always, but at each *now* of my prayer, I should remember in a special way those who have asked me to pray for them or those whom I know need my help on this unique and passing day of the world's history, including them all in my prayer at the word *now*.

And at the hour of our death Again remembering all, because all of us who live must die, and must meet our merciful God in his judgement of love that no one can escape, not even those who now know nothing about it.

Basis of the method

In this method of praying the Rosary, we address the words of the Hail Mary to Mary as she was when she lived though the events of each particular mystery, so that the words we say take on new meanings in different mysteries. Thus, 'blessed are you' and 'blessed is Jesus' will obviously have different applications to Mary in the stable, and to Mary on Calvary.

How to pray the rosary

Scripture readings

The words therefore are not just recited *before* Mary; they are addressed *to* her. In order to address them to her in the particular decade we are saying, we should know clearly her part in each of the fifteen events of salvation history found in the traditional mysteries of the Rosary. A short descriptive sentence is therefore added to each title, with references to help us find suitable scripture readings for each mystery.

The suggested readings either describe the event, or show how the apostles used it in their preaching, or (as especially in the case of the Assumption and the Coronation, which are not recorded in scripture) give some teaching or thoughts connected with the mystery. Sometimes, one of these readings could be read — perhaps before each mystery at longer group prayer meetings, or before one mystery of the family Rosary.

Some phrases changed

The new feature of this method is that at times we change the two phrases, 'full of grace' and 'the Lord is with thee' in order to help us remember more explicitly Mary's particular part in each mystery.

These phrases were first addressed by the angel Gabriel to Mary at the Annunciation, and hundreds of generations have found them valid for other events of her life also.

However, we know that God gave Mary many different graces or gifts at different moments of her life.

The left hand columns of pages 180-188 contain, in capitals, suggestions for alternative phrases to be substituted for the phrase 'full of grace' in different mysteries, to express more explicitly the particular 'graces' Mary received in different events of her life.

The right hand columns contain phrases which may be used as alternatives to 'the Lord is with thee', to express more clearly some particular way that 'the Lord' (Father, Son or Holy Spirit) was 'with' Mary in the events of each mystery.

At the head of each column the phrases 'full of grace' and 'the Lord is with you', remind us that these are omitted when the phrases underneath are used.

This method is used by adding to the traditional opening words 'Hail Mary', one of the new phrases taken from each column of the mystery being prayed and then completing it with the traditional words, 'blessed are you, etc...' Even without change in these latter words, you will find that their meaning and application will be changed in each of the different mysteries, according as different substitute phrases are used in the first part of the prayer.

Group use

This method should not be introduced to members of a family or group unless they first understand and approve the experiment. *The leader alone* is required to change phrases, and he/she should prepare them — and the readings if desired — beforehand, to avoid hesitancy that distracts, and to ensure that a combination of phrases suitable for the group is chosen. There should not be more than a few changes in each mystery, to allow sufficient time for each phrase chosen to sink into people's minds, and to avoid the distraction that too many changes may cause.

'Blessed is Jesus'

The Hail Mary is not a prayer of praise and petition to Mary alone. We honour her because her Son, Jesus Christ, is God. We should remember that the Hail Mary also includes an explicit prayer of praise for Jesus, in the phrase, 'blessed is the fruit of your womb, Jesus'. Perhaps we seldom think of this because in group use the response often starts so quickly that the final word, the name 'Jesus', is not heard!

To avoid this, it is sometimes useful to change the order of words in this phrase to the following: 'blessed is Jesus, the fruit of your womb'. The clear and constant repetition of the phrase 'blessed is Jesus' makes it impossible to forget that Jesus is really and explicitly praised in each Hail Mary of the rosary.

A shorter rosary

When people do not have time for the whole rosary, they sometimes omit one or more mysteries, or omit a few Hail Marys from each mystery.

Another alternative is to shorten each Hail Mary as described below, retaining what is most important and thus emphasising our basic approach and prayer to Jesus and Mary.

The leader will say the first two phrases of the Hail Mary, choosing, where desired, different phrases as suggested later in this section, while all the rest of the prayer is shortened and said as the response by the others sharing in that Rosary...

Thus after the leader says:

> Hail Mary, full of grace, the Lord is with you, *or*
> Hail Mary, full of love, Jesus lives in you, *or*
> Hail Mary, full of pain, standing by the cross, *or*
> Hail Mary, full of joy, Christ now lives again, *etc*

the others respond:

> Blessed is Jesus, blessed are you.
> Pray for us sinners, now and at death.

Singing the new version

The new phrases suggested on pp. 180-188 have been kept, as far as possible, to the same length and rhythm — with for example, the words 'Christ', 'Jesus', or 'your Son' being chosen in different phrases for this reason.

This makes the phrases easier to memorise. It also makes it possible to use them in place of the italic words in the prayer verse below, which can be sung to the tune of 'Soul of my Saviour' or some other similar suitable tune. This could perhaps be done in group use for the last one or two Hail Marys of each decade, with the leader or cantor singing the first line with the chosen phrases, and others joining in the last three unchanging lines which are easily memorized.

(Tune: Soul of my Saviour)

Hail Mary, *full of grace, God lives with you.*

Blessed of women, — praised be Christ your son.
Hail, holy Mary, mother of our God,
Pra-ay for us sinners, now and as we die.

Repeating each phrase

As an additional variation for use when alone, we could sometimes repeat each phrase of the Hail Mary ten times before going on to the next — instead of saying the whole prayer ten times as at present. This enables the mind to dwell more fully on each phrase in the context of the mystery and to discover new depths of meaning in these phrases we so often repeat without thinking of their meaning.

Conclusion

It is not intended that this should be 'the new rosary', to take the place of the indulgenced official version. But it has been found that occasional use of this method makes our usual rosary more prayerful, as we remember the different meanings and applications we can give to the traditional phrases we are using.

THE FIVE JOYFUL MYSTERIES

(Sundays of Advent and Christmas, Mondays, Thursdays)

Here I can pray specially for
FAITH
in the Son of God
who became man and entered this world,
at a particular moment of its history.

1 The Annunciation

God sends Gabriel to tell Mary she is to be the mother of his Son, who takes flesh in her womb when she accepts God's plan.

> Genesis 3:8-15 (Redemption foretold)
> Luke 1:26-38 (Story of Annunciation)
> Matthew 1:18-25 (An Angel tells Joseph)
> Isaiah 7:10-14 (Virgin conception foretold)
> John 1:1-28 (The Word was made flesh)
> Philippians 2:1-11 (Jesus empties himself)

(full of grace)	*(the Lord is with you)*
FULL OF JOY,	you believe God's word.
FULL OF FAITH,	saying 'yes' to God.
FULL OF LOVE,	you accept God's plan.
CHOSEN ONE,	Christ takes flesh in you.
SECOND EVE,	Jesus lives in you.
VIRGIN PURE,	Christ becomes your Son.

The Joyful Mysteries

2 The Visitation

Mary, with Jesus in her womb, goes to visit and help Elizabeth, pregnant with John who is to prepare the way for Jesus, and praises God for his gifts to her.

>Luke 1:39-45 (Mary visits Elizabeth)
>Luke 1:46-56 (Mary praises the Lord)

(full of grace)	*(the Lord is with you)*
FULL OF JOY,	glad to help your friends.
FULL OF LOVE,	Christ is in your womb.
HUMBLE, KIND,	Jesus loves in you.
TEACHING LOVE,	Jesus helps you serve.
FULL OF FAITH,	praised by Holy Spirit.
VIRGIN PURE,	singing thanks to God.

3 The Nativity

Mary gives birth to Jesus in a stable and shows him to shepherds and kings.

>Luke 2:1-7 (Birth of Jesus)
>Luke 2:8-17 (Angels and Shepherds)
>Matthew 2:1-12 (The Kings from the East)
>Romans 1:1-5 (Born a descendant of David)
>Galatians 4:1-7 (Son of a human mother)
>2 Corinthians 8:1-9 (Christ made himself poor for you)

(full of grace)	*(the Lord is with you)*
FULL OF JOY,	giving birth to Christ.
FULL OF LOVE,	angels praise your Son.
FULL OF FAITH,	watching Christ with love.
FULL OF HOPE,	nursing Christ your Son.
FULL OF THANKS,	poor with Christ your Son.
HAPPY MOTHER,	showing Christ to men.

4 The Presentation

Mary offers her Son to God in the temple where Simeon and Anna worship him, and tell Mary she will suffer.

>Luke 2:22-24 & 39-40   (Jesus is offered)
>Luke 2:25-38   (Simeon and Anna)

(full of grace)	*(the Lord is with you)*
FULL OF JOY,	worshipping the Lord.
FULL OF LOVE,	praying in God's house.
FULL OF FAITH,	offering Christ to God.
HOLY MOTHER,	showing Christ to saints.
HOLY, GLAD,	accepting future pain.
FULL OF TRUST,	keeping the Law of God.

5 The Finding in the Temple

Losing the twelve year old Jesus in Jerusalem for three days, Mary and Joseph find him in the temple, and they all return to live in their home at Nazareth.

>Luke 2:41-50   (Jesus is lost and found)
>Luke 2:51-52   (The hidden life at Nazareth)

(full of grace)	*(the Lord is with you)*
FULL OF FAITH,	you keep the Pasch with Christ.
FULL OF HOPE,	seeking Christ your Son.
FULL OF LOVE,	finding Christ your Son.
TEACHING LOVE,	Christ goes home with you.
FULL OF JOY,	Christ obeys your words.
GRATEFUL MOTHER,	watching Christ grow up.

THE FIVE SORROWFUL MYSTERIES

(Sundays of Lent, Tuesdays and Fridays)

Here we can specially pray for
LOVE
for Jesus Christ, who died for me,
and for all his people whom he loved even to death.

1 The Agony in the Garden

Mary hears of the agony Christ suffered as he foresees and prepares for his passion.

Matthew 26:36-46; Mark 14:32-42; Luke 22:39-46
(The agony of Jesus described)
Mathew 26:47-56; Mark 14:43-50; Luke 22:47-53
(The capture of Jesus described)
Matthew 17:22-23   (Christ foretells his death)

(full of grace)	*(the Lord is with you)*
GRIEVED AND SAD,	told of Christ's distress.
FULL OF SORROW,	Christ foresees his death.
PAINED IN SOUL,	Christ is crushed by fear.
FULL OF LOVE,	Christ's sweat falls like blood.
FULL OF GRIEF,	Christ accepts God's will.
MOTHER SAD,	told of Christ's arrest.

2 The Scourging at the Pillar

Mary hears that Christ was scourged by the Roman soldiers.

> Luke 23:13-15 & Matthew 27:15-26 (Scourging)
> Matthew 20:17-19 (Christ foretells the scourging)
> Hebrews 5:5-10 (Obedient by his suffering)
> Hebrews 9:11-14 (Jesus saved us by his own blood)

(full of grace)	*(the Lord is with you)*
FULL OF SORROW,	Christ is scourged and bleeds.
GRIEVED AND SAD,	hearing Christ was scourged.
WEEPING TEARS,	Christ unjustly judged.
CRUSHED IN GRIEF,	Christ condemned to die.
FULL OF LOVE,	men rejected Christ.
PAINED IN HEART,	Jesus bleeds for us.

3 The Crowning with Thorns

Mary hears that Christ was crowned with thorns and mocked by the Roman soldiers.

> Matthew 27:27-31 (Account of the crowning)
> Isaiah 53:1-7 (Despised and rejected)
> Psalm 22(21):1-15 (A worm and no man)

(full of grace)	*(the Lord is with you)*
FULL OF SORROW	Christ is in your thoughts.
PAINED IN SOUL,	Christ is crowned with thorns.
SAD AND WEEPING,	hearing Christ was mocked.
BROKEN-HEARTED,	Christ is hurt by pride.
FULL OF LOVE,	sinners laugh at Christ.
CRUSHED IN GRIEF,	Christ is shamed by men.

The Sorrowful Mysteries

4 The Carrying of the Cross

Mary meets Jesus, and watches him suffer, as he carries his cross to Calvary.

> Luke 23:26-31 (The journey to Calvary)
> Mark 8:31-38 (He must carry his cross)
> Philippians 2:1-11 (He walked the path to death)
> Hebrews 12:1-4 (He endured the cross)

(full of grace)   *(the Lord is with you)*
SHARING PAIN,   Christ accepts his cross.
FULL OF SORROW,   meeting Christ your Son.
PAINED IN SOUL,   seeing wounds of Christ.
FULL OF LOVE,   watching Christ collapse.
BROKEN-HEARTED,   glad Christ's face is wiped.
PATIENT MOTHER,   Simon helps your Son.

5 The Crucifixion

Mary accepts her suffering as she watches Christ die after three hours on the cross.

> Matthew 27:32-56; Luke 23:32-49; John 19:17-30 (Calvary)
> Ephesians 5:1-5 (Christ gave his life for us)
> Romans 5:6-11 (Christ died for us)
> 1 Corinthians 1:18-25 (We preach Christ crucified)
> 1 Peter 1:13-23 (Freed by Christ's blood)
> Galatians 2:19-3:3 (Crucified with Christ)

(full of grace)   *(the Lord is with you)*
CALLED TO SUFFER,   standing by the cross.
SHARING PAIN,   hearing nails being struck.
FULL OF PAIN,   watching Christ in pain.
WEEPING TEARS,   watching Christ in death.
FULL OF LOVE,   one with Christ in love.
FULL OF FAITH,   offering Christ to God.

THE FIVE GLORIOUS MYSTERIES

(All other Sundays of the year, Wednesdays, Saturdays)

Here I can pray specially for
HOPE
as I look forward to the eternal life promised by Jesus.

1 The Resurrection

Christ rises from the dead and meets his mother and the disciples.
(*Note:* The details of his personal meeting with his mother are not recorded).

> Luke 24:1-12; John 20:1-10 (Empty tomb)
> John 20:11-18 (Mary Magdalene)
> John 20:19-29 (Disciples and Thomas)
> Luke 24:13-35 (The road to Emmaus)
> 1 Corinthians 15:1-11 & 20-23 (Christ is risen)
> Acts 2:22-24 & 32-42 (We give witness)
> Acts 10:34-43 (God raised him from death)
> Colossians 3:1-4 (You are raised with Christ)

(full of grace)	*(the Lord is with you)*
FULL OF JOY,	Christ arose from death.
PRAISING GOD,	meeting risen Christ.
HAPPY, GLAD,	meeting Christ alive.
THANKING GOD,	Christ now lives again.
FULL OF LOVE,	Christ shows he's divine.
JOYFUL MOTHER,	Christ who died now lives.

The Glorious Mysteries

2 The Ascension

Saying farewell to his mother and his apostles, Jesus returns to his Father in heaven.

>   Luke 24:49-53; Acts 1:1-11   (Ascension)
>   John 14:1-6   ('I go to prepare a place')
>   John 16:16-22   ('I am going to my Father')
>   Ephesians 4:7-13   (He ascended to send gifts)
>   Hebrews 8:1-6   (Jesus in heaven as our priest)
>   Hebrews 12:1-4   (Encouraged by the ascension)

(full of grace)	*(the Lord is with you)*
FULL OF FAITH,	Christ ascends to heaven.
FULL OF HOPE,	Christ completes his work.
FULL OF LOVE,	Christ leaves you on earth.
THANKING GOD,	sad when Christ departs.
PRAISING GOD,	lonely for your Son.
HOLY MOTHER,	Christ will send his Spirit.

3 The descent of the Holy Spirit

The Holy Spirit comes on Mary and the apostles and the Church grows.

>   Acts 1:12-14   (Mary prays with the twelve)
>   Acts 2:1-4 & 40-42   (Pentecost day)
>   John 14:15-26   (Another helper promised)
>   John 16:4-15   (Spirit of truth to teach us)

(full of grace)	*(the Lord is with you)*
FULL OF JOY,	praying with the twelve.
THANKING GOD,	working with Christ's Church.
FULL OF LOVE,	helping Church to spread.
PRAISING GOD,	the Spirit fills your soul.
SERVING GOD,	the Spirit comes to you.
STRONG IN FAITH,	full of the Spirit of Christ.

4 The Assumption into Heaven

Jesus takes Mary his mother, body and soul, to eternal happiness in heaven.

> Genesis 3:14-15 (Mary at war with the devil)
> Revelation 21:1-8 (God will be with them)
> 1 Corinthians 15:35-57 (Death is destroyed)
> 2 Corinthians 5:1-10 (Our home with the Lord)
> 1 Corinthians 13:8-13 (Seeing God face to face)
> 1 John 3:1-3 (Seeing God as he really is)

(full of grace)	*(the Lord is with you)*
FULL OF GLORY,	face to face with Christ.
FULL OF LOVE,	seeing Christ as God.
GLAD IN HEAVEN,	sharing God's true life.
FULL OF BLISS,	knowing as God knows.
LOVING US,	one with God through Christ.
STILL OUR MOTHER,	body and soul with Christ.

5 The Coronation

Jesus crowns Mary as Queen of heaven, next to him in the glory of God.

> Colossians 1:9-14 (Safe in Christ's kingdom)
> Colossians 1:15-20 (Christ, the first-born Son)
> Colossians 3:1-4 (You will share his glory)
> 1 Corinthians 15:20-28 (Each in his proper order)
> Ephesians 1:17-23 (Christ rules in heaven)

(full of grace)	*(the Lord is with you)*
FULL OF GLORY,	Jesus crowns you Queen.
SEEING GOD,	Queen for evermore.
GLAD FOR EVER,	next to Christ your Son.
LOVING GOD,	Mother of our King.
FULL OF JOY,	life eternal's yours.
ONE WITH GOD,	Mother of the Church.

Marian Devotions for Today

Novena to Our Lady, Mother of the Church

This section contains the teaching of Vatican Two on Our Lady, as contained in chapter 8 of the Constitution on the Church. This guarantees an accurate and up to date presentation of Our Lady's place in the history of salvation; while its rearrangement in prayer form, addressed to God and to Our Lady, will ensure that its truths will easily and naturally become part of the daily lives of those who use it regularly.

The number in brackets after each prayer heading gives the reference to the relevant paragraph of chapter 8 of the Constitution on the Church.

Suggestions for alternative choices for public use (e.g. May devotions, weekly novena, prayer group), in a service lasting about twenty minutes including a three minute homily, are given on pages 192, 197, 199, 200, 201.

'Let the faithful remember
that true devotion to the Blessed Virgin consists
neither in sterile or passing feelings,
nor in vain credulity,
but proceeds from true faith,
by which we are led to recognise
the excellence of the Mother of God,
and we are moved to a filial love towards our mother,
and to the imitation of her virtues'

(Constitution on the Church, 66)

Opening prayer (66)

Almighty Father, we offer these prayers/this novena to honour the blessed Virgin Mary. You honoured her next to your Son, and more than all the angels and saints, because you chose her to be the most holy Mother of God, and to take a special part in the life and work of Christ.

In these prayers, we honour and love her, we call on her help, and we promise to imitate her. Thus we fulfill her prophecy, 'All generations will call me blessed, because he who is mighty has done great things for me.'

While honouring the mother of Christ, we pray that her Son may be fittingly known, loved and glorified, and all his commandments faithfully followed. For through him all things were created, and in him it has pleased you to let all fullness dwell.

I. 'WE HONOUR AND LOVE HER'

Prayer of praise (53)

O Mary, virgin and mother, when the angel told you that you were to be the mother of God, you welcomed the Word of God in your heart and in your body, and gave Life to the world. We therefore praise and honour you as the true mother of God our Redeemer.

Because of the merits of your Son, you were redeemed in a special manner, you were united to Christ in a close and lasting union, and you were given the high privilege of being the mother of the Son of God, the favourite daughter of the Father, and the resting place of the Holy Spirit.

Because of this wonderful gift of love and grace, you surpass all other creatures of God, whether in heaven or on earth. You are indeed a child of Adam, and so, like us, you needed to be redeemed. Yet you are clearly the mother of the members of Christ, because you co-operated through love that children might be born in the Church, who would be members of Christ its head.

We salute you, therefore, as the most special member of the Church and as our outstanding model of faith and love. Led by the Holy Spirit, we offer you our love, the love of children to their most lovable mother.

Litany of praise (55-59) Week 1

(For public use, choose one page from pp. 192-195 each time)

Hail Mary, foreshadowed in the promise of victory
made to our first parents after their fall into sin:

Response
   Blessed are you among women.
   Blessed is Jesus, the fruit of your womb.

Hail, Mary, foretold by the prophet
as the virgin who was to conceive and bear a son:

Hail, Mary, outstanding member
of God's poor and humble people,
who waited in hope for the coming of his salvation:

Hail, Mary, the long waiting of your people for a Saviour
was rewarded through you,
when your Son established
the new covenant between God and man:

Hail, Mary, the Son of God took human nature from you,
to free mankind from sin,
through the mysteries of his flesh:

Hail, Mary, it was the Father's will
that your free consent be given
before the Incarnation took place:

Hail, Mary, it was the Father's will
that as a woman contributed to our death,
so also a woman should contribute to bringing us life:

Hail, Mary, enriched by God with gifts
to make you worthy of this great privilege:

Hail, Mary, praised by the Fathers of the Church
as completely holy, and free from every trace of sin:

Hail, Mary, made so holy by the Holy Spirit,
that you were, as it were, formed into a new creature:

I. We honour and love her

Week 2

Hail, Mary, enriched from the moment of your
conception, with a holiness no one else enjoyed:

Response
> **Blessed are you among women.**
> **Blessed is Jesus, the fruit of your womb.**

Hail, Mary, virgin of Nazareth,
God commanded his angel to call you 'full of grace':

Hail, Mary, replying to God's messenger in the words:
'I am the handmaid of the Lord,
let it be done to me according to your will.'

Hail, Mary, in these words accepting God's invitation,
you were made the mother of Jesus:

Hail, Mary, gladly embracing God's plan to save us,
you offered yourself
with the love of your sinless heart,
to the service of your Son and his work:

Hail, Mary, you were allowed,
through the love of the all-powerful God,
to share in the work of our Redemption,
in union with your Son, and dependent on him:

Hail, Mary, by your free response of faith and obedience,
you actively co-operated in the work of our salvation:

Hail, Mary, through your obedience,
you were made a source of salvation
for yourself and for the whole human race:

Hail, Mary, untying through your obedience
the knot of Eve's disobedience,
and loosening through your faith,
what Eve had bound through her unbelief:

Hail, Mary, mother of the living,
through whom life came to us,
just as death came to us through Eve:

Hail, Mary, united to your Son in his saving work
from the time of his conception to his death:

Response
>Blessed are you among women.
>Blessed is Jesus, the fruit of your womb.

Hail, Mary, when you visited Elizabeth,
she greeted you as blessed,
because of your faith in the Saviour promised by God:

Hail, Mary, as soon as you greeted Elizabeth,
her son, John the Baptist, leaped with joy in her womb:

Hail, Mary, mother of God, you gave birth to your Son
while remaining a virgin:

Hail, Mary, mother of God, after the birth of your Son,
you joyfully showed him to shepherds and kings:

Hail, Mary, you presented your Son to the Lord
in the temple, making there the offering of the poor:

Hail, Mary, you heard Simeon foretell,
that your Son would be rejected by many,
and that a sword would pierce your soul:

Hail, Mary, after three days' search for your Son,
you found him in the temple,
engaged in his Father's work:

Hail, Mary, you were moved with pity
at the marriage feast of Cana of Galilee,
and at your request,
Jesus the Messiah began his life of miracles:

Hail, Mary, listening to your Son
when he declared 'blessed'
all those who heard and kept his word:

Hail, Mary, faithfully united to your Son
throughout your whole life of faith:

I. We honour and love her

Hail, Mary, standing by the cross on Calvary,
because God willed it,
you suffered grievously with your only Son:

Response
   Blessed are you among women.
   Blessed is Jesus, the fruit of your womb.

Hail, Mary, uniting yourself with a mother's love,
to the sacrifice of your Son,
you consented for love of us to the death of the victim
who had been born of you:

Hail, Mary, when Christ Jesus was dying,
he gave you as mother to his disciple, John,
in the words, 'Woman, behold your Son':

Hail, Mary, blessed above all after the Resurrection,
in your joy at meeting your Son, the risen Christ:

Hail, Mary, seeing in the risen body of Christ,
the glory that awaited you after your Assumption:

Hail, Mary, seeing in his risen body
the glory that God has in store for us on the last day,
when the Son will hand back the kingdom to his Father:

Hail, Mary, after the Ascension,
you prayed with the apostles,
for the promised coming of the Spirit,
through whom the Church, the sign of human salvation,
was to be shown forth to the world:

Hail, Mary, immaculate Virgin,
kept free from every stain of original sin,
at the end of your life on earth
you were taken up body and soul into heavenly glory:

Hail, Mary, raised by God as Queen of all,
so as to have a closer likeness to your Son,
who is King of Kings, the conqueror of sin and death:

Homily

On one of the Salvation History events listed in the preceding Litany.

Hymn of praise (52)

Suggested tune: OLD LOURDES Hymn

1 God sent his own Son, of a woman to be born,
   That we might receive the adoption of sons.
   Ave, ave, ave, Maria. Ave, ave, ave, Maria.

2 Christ came down from heaven to save us from sin,
   Through power of the Spirit, of Virgin conceived.
   Ave, ave, ave, Maria. Ave, ave, ave, Maria.

3 Believers in Christ, with his saints we sing your praise,
   The mother of Jesus our God and our Lord.
   Ave, ave, ave, Maria. Ave, ave, ave, Maria.

II 'WE CALL ON HER FOR HELP'

Special intentions

Announcement of special needs for which prayers are requested may be inserted either here or after the following prayer.

Prayer for Help (60-61) Weeks 1 and 3

(For public use, choose either this or the following page)

O Mary, we ask your help with confidence. We know that there is one mediator between God and man, Christ Jesus, who gave himself as a ransom for all. But the motherly help we receive from you does not lessen or take anything away from the one and only mediation of Christ, but rather shows its powers.

Your power to help us is not something necessary; it arises from the completely free choice of God, it flows from the abundant merits of Christ, it is wholly dependent on his mediation, and draws all its strength from it. The help we ask from you will strengthen our close union with Christ.

O Blessed Virgin Mary, from all eternity, you were a part of God's plan for the Incarnation of his Son, the divine Word. From all eternity, the providence of God chose you for existence, as the mother of the Redeemer, as the humble servant of the Lord, and as his unselfish companion and friend, closer to him than any other.

You conceived, brought forth, and nourished Christ. You presented him to the Father in the Temple. You suffered with him as he died on the cross. During your whole life, through your obedience, faith, hope and burning love, you co-operated more than anyone else in the world, in our Saviour's work of redemption.

You are indeed truly our mother, in the kingdom of God's love, and we come to you confidently for help.

Prayer for the Church and for unity (68-69)   *Weeks 2 and 4*

O Mary, Mother of Jesus, the glory of body and soul you now possess in heaven shows us the happiness that we will enjoy when the Church reaches her perfect state in the world to come. As long as life remains in this world, you shine forth from heaven, as the sign of sure hope and comfort for the people of God on their pilgrimage.

We are glad to be united with all Christians who give fitting honour to you, as the mother of Our Lord and Saviour, and especially with the Eastern Christians, who have always honoured you with such great love and devotion.

With all believers in Christ, we pour out urgent and constant prayers to you for the whole church. As you gave support with your prayers, when the Church began its life of service on earth, and as you are now raised above all your fellow members of the Church glorious in heaven, pray to your Son for us as we live and work in that same Church today.

Continue to pray for us, until all people in the world, Christians and those who do not yet know Christ, are happily gathered in peace and unity, into the one people of God, for the glory of the most holy and undivided Trinity.

II. We call on her for help

Litany for help

Weeks 1 and 3

(*For public use, choose either 1 or 2*)

1

Holy Mary, becoming our mother at the Annunciation, in the consent which you gave through faith:

Response
**Blessed is Jesus, blessed are you.
Pray for us sinners, now and at death.**

Holy Mary, still our mother at the foot of the cross, where your sufferings for us did not weaken your motherly love:

Holy Mary, our mother as long as we live, even to the perfect happiness of heaven:

Holy Mary, still our mother after you were taken up to heaven, you continue to obtain for us by your prayers, the gifts of divine friendship and love:

Holy Mary, with motherly love you care for us, who call your Son our brother and who still journey through the dangers and sorrows of this life:

2 *Weeks 2 and 4*

Holy Mary, our Advocate, our Defender, our Helper, our Patron:

Holy Mary, we know that in asking your help, we neither take away from nor add to the dignity and power of Christ, our one Mediator:

Holy Mary, you share in a special way in the mediatorship of Christ, just as all creatures share in the one goodness of God:

Holy Mary, you share in a special way in the mediatorship of Christ, just as priests and people share in his priesthood:

Holy Mary, your power is dependent on that of your Son, but you can still help us so much that we ask you to help us all to be more closely united to Christ our Mediator and our Saviour.

Hymn for help (61, 62, 58)

Suggested Tune: Hail, Queen of Heaven
(*For public use: two verses each time*)
       Week 1: verses 1 and 2; *Week 2:* verses 2 and 3 etc.

1. Hail, Mother of Christ, and our mother too,
   you worked with Christ to bring life to our souls:
   through faith, hope and love, obedient to God,
   you are our mother in God's loving plan.
   Mother of Christ, our mother too,
   pray for us all who call upon you.

2. Hail, Mother of Christ, and our mother too,
   since you agreed to be mother of God,
   accepting the Lord, your motherly love
   gathered us all as your children with him.

3. Hail, Mother of Christ, your love grew no less,
   as by the cross you watched Jesus in pain;
   to heaven raised up, you keep your love strong,
   help us at all times with motherly prayers.

4. Hail, Mother of Christ, with motherly love,
   care for us all who are brethren of Christ,
   we travel, through life, amidst many trials,
   lead us all safe to our heavenly home.

5. Hail, Mother of Christ, at Cana your prayers
   led Jesus Christ to change water to wine;
   remember our needs, and pray that your Son,
   grant all we need for our life every day.

III 'WE PROMISE TO IMITATE HER'

(For public use: choose either this or the next page)

Mary our model (63-64)   *Weeks 1 and 3*

Most blessed Virgin Mary, Mother of God, your life of faith and love in perfect unity with Christ, was planned by God to show us clearly what our lives should be. Within the life of the Church, herself rightly called Mother and Virgin, you are the outstanding model of motherhood and virginity.

You are the mother of God, O Mary, for through faith and obedience, you gave birth to the Son of the Father. And you are our spiritual mother also, for the Son you brought forth is placed as the first-born among many brethren, the faithful people of God in whose birth and growth you help with motherly love.

Accepting God's work in faith, the Church also becomes a mother. For through her preaching and baptism she brings forth to a new and immortal life children who are conceived of the Holy Spirit and born of God.

Help us all to understand that we will fulfill this work more perfectly, O Holy Mother, by trying to understand the secret of your holiness, and by imitating your love, and your obedience to God's will.

Holy Mary, in your motherhood you remained a virgin, for you brought forth your Son, not through the power of man, but through the power of the Holy Spirit, when you consented to the messenger of God with your whole heart and strength.

The Church is also a virgin, who wholeheartedly keeps perfect the faithful love she has promised her spouse. Help each of us, O Virgin Mother of God, to accept like you the power of the Holy Spirit, and to serve you with our whole heart, in full faith, in firm hope, and in unselfish love.

Prayer to imitate Mary (65)   Weeks 2 and 4

In you, most holy virgin, the Church has already reached that perfection by which she will live in glory without stain or wrinkle. We, your fellow members in the Church, and believers in Christ, are still fighting to overcome sin and to grow in holiness and love. Help us to fix our mind on you, Mary, for you are the perfect example of all the virtues, for us who hope for salvation. As we remember you, and let our minds rest with love on your life of loving union with the Word made Flesh, our lives will be more deeply changed by the mystery of the Incarnation, and we will grow more and more like our divine Redeemer.

O Mary, it was God's will in the long story of his loving plan for our salvation, that your life would show forth for us the central truths of our faith. So when you are preached and honoured today, you call those who believe to your Son, to his redeeming sacrifice, and to the Father's love. May we grow more like you our holy Model, in giving glory to Christ, in growing always in faith, hope and love, and in seeking and doing the will of God in all things.

We look especially for your example in our apostolic work. You brought forth Christ, conceived by the Holy Spirit, and born of your virginal body, so that through our work in the Church, he might be born and grow also in the hearts of those who believe in him. Help us to imitate the example you gave us during your whole life, of that unselfish motherly love, which should fill the souls of all who work in the Church to bring new life to men.

The Communion of Saints

St Paul: 'As for us, we have this large crowd of witnesses round us. So then, let us rid ourselves of everything that gets in the way, and of the sin which holds on to us so tightly, and let us run with determination the race that lies before us... keeping our eyes fixed on Jesus...'   (Hebrews 12:1,2)

REFLECTION ON THE SAINTS

How do the saints know us?

The saints we pray to were united to Christ when they died, and so they have entered with him into the life of the Blessed Trinity. In some way we cannot understand, they 'share in the divine nature of God'. They see the living God 'as he really is' — his wisdom, his power, his love, his providence. They know us therefore with God's knowledge, as God knows us, and they love us with *his* love, as he loves us. (cf. 1 Cor 13:8-12, 1 John 3:1-3, 2 Peter 1:3-4).

This is the only way that they can now know you and me. Of their own human power alone they cannot know us any better after death than they did before death!

If, while they were still alive, a friend asked their help, they could not hear him if they were too far away. They would have to be close enough to hear him before they could listen and respond... And even then they could listen and reply to only one person at a time...

After their death, they still live, but now they see God face to face, and know him as he really is, even as he knows them. Knowing him and his providence, they know our requests, not by hearing with their human ears and knowing them with their human minds, but 'in God', as he knows each one of us in every detail of our personal individual lives, our unspoken thoughts and silent prayers as well as those we put into words. They know and love us in God, only because God knows and loves us, and they share in that knowledge and love. When we turn to them in praise or petition, they experience our prayer in God — but they do so as separate individual persons, each distinct from God, yet each living 'in him'.

Our prayer to them is an act of faith in God's word that they are alive and living — and an expression of our hope that they are in heaven, where they live, not with a human life limited by time and space, in which they could not hear us if they were not close to us and listening to us, but where they live in God, sharing God's life and knowing with his knowledge and love.

Why do we pray to saints?

Our prayers *to the saints* are therefore really acts of love and praise and petition *to God*, in whom they live, through whom they hear us, and without whom they could not hear us.

We pray to them not because they can help us more than God can, nor because they want to help us more than God does, but because they are men and women like ourselves who lived human lives in this world, people whom perhaps we learned to know well either in person, or from the words or writings of others. And so, we sometimes find it easier and more natural and more human to go to God 'through them', than to go to God directly. We are easily drawn to friendship, love and trust towards people whose love and goodness we personally experienced in the past, or people who faced and overcame difficulties and temptations like ours — people who, like us, sinned and were forgiven, people whose lives remind us that we, like them, are called to the destiny of sharing God's life when we leave this world in his friendship.

Prayer to saints honours God

We go to God the Father through Christ his Son, who became one of us to make it easier for us to know and approach the Father through him. So also the saints, united to Christ as they lived and died in this world, are now united with Christ in heaven. We can go to God the Father not merely through Christ, the second Person of the Trinity made man, but through people in heaven who are part of the Body of Christ, people living in Christ and with Christ, people united to him as living branches are united to a vine, people who have become in a sense 'other Christs', whom we indeed know with our human minds, but who know and respond to us through the inner life of the Trinity which they share with Christ.

In the order of our consciousness, we can indeed and correctly approach God through his saints, but in reality we are approaching the saint through God, who is the only effective link between us. 'To Jesus through Mary' is a valid, and for some a useful, way of consciously approaching God. But 'to Mary through God' is the way we really go!

Who are saints?

But how do we know who are 'saints'? How do we know what people are in heaven, able to hear us when we pray to them? This is important, because if the person we pray to is not sharing God's life in heaven, he cannot even hear our prayers, much less respond to them.

We cannot directly know who is in heaven until we reach there ourselves when, in knowing God 'face to face', we will also know all those united to him. In the meantime, there are many people whom we can reasonably judge are in heaven either because of our personal knowledge of them, or because of what others told us about them, people about whom we can humanly say: 'If they are not in heaven then there is nobody there, and our faith and lives are in vain!' We can pray to them as a personal and private act, using our own personal judgement and opinion; but, as this may be mistaken we are not allowed to offer any public or official reverence to them on this basis alone.

And then we have people who are called 'saints' in the strict sense. These are people who were first considered saints by their friends who, as mentioned above, personally experienced and knew their holiness, and were convinced that they were in heaven. These were later declared 'saints' by the Church, after she had investigated the details of their lives and the effect their writing and example had on other people, the benefits received by those who imitated them, and the favours and miracles God granted to people who prayed to them. This process ended with a formal 'canonization', in which the Church formally declared that this holy person was indeed in heaven, and allowed, and in fact encouraged, us to honour him/her publicly in prayer and devotion. These are the canonized 'saints', the people whom our Church assures us are in heaven, so that we can publicly praise them, imitate them and ask their help, confident because of our Church's authority, that they share God's life and therefore, can hear and answer us through God's knowledge and power.

Each alight with Christ

The saints are 'friends'

We have all experienced 'friendship'. But also, most of us have sometimes felt sorrow at the imperfection or loss of human friendship, at the occasional difficulties of showing love to someone we love very much, at misunderstanding and quarrels with friends, at the pain of separation through emigration or death. But our faith tells us that those who have died in God can still be our friends, with a friendship and love that is stronger than it was in this world, because they know us now with God's love and friendship and therefore know our love for them, a love made known to them in this world only occasionally and imperfectly.

And knowing us as God knows us, they know us as we really are, with our secret sins and selfishness, our weakness and hypocrisy. They really know us in a way we would not want them (or anyone else) to know us *in this world*, because merely human love would seldom be strong enough to enable them to love us when they know us in all our sins and weaknesses! They share in God's life, and as he loves us in spite of our sins and forgives us when we turn back to him — even seventy times seven times — so do they.

We still turn to them with a human love, but with a human love now changed by our hope that they are in heaven, and by our faith that in the new life of heaven, they know and love us in a new way.

Billions of friends!

After death, we will know not merely the friends and people we met in this world, but also all our other friends, all our 'brothers and sisters' — some of whom we have met briefly in this life, some of whom we may have heard of, but the vast majority of whom we have neither known nor heard of. These are the countless millions living today — the thousands we see daily in our streets, or in photos of religious, sporting or political gatherings — and the countless people of past centuries and of the (perhaps thousands) of centuries to come. All are individual unique lovable people, whom God created, or will create, in his image and likeness, to know and love him. All belong to the same race to whose welfare, to whose salvation — and at times to whose very existence — we contribute by our actions. They belong to that same race to which we belong with Jesus and Mary, with Adam and Eve, with Herod and Pilate, with Hitler and Stalin... to the race, which is 'our human race' and which would be a different 'human race', or a race of different humans, if even one of us were absent! To get to know them individually and share their different and unique lives would take too many millions of years of human 'time' for this world to contain. So God planned heaven as an endless eternity where 'time' will not limit our loves and our joys.

And each of these billions and billions of individual persons is worth knowing, because each is made in the image of God. Each of them is worth loving because each is loved by God who knows them personally and intimately. Each of them is capable of giving joy and happiness through the friendship of his/her individual person, because each has been created by God to find full fulfilment in loving others as well as loving him.

Our friendship and resulting joy will be far greater in heaven with these billions than any happiness we can experience with our nearest and dearest in this world. Because there we can know each 'other', not superficially and from outside as in this world, but intimately and completely, sharing and experiencing with them each moment of their lives, each joy and each sorrow, every excitement and every boredom, every success and every failure, every pleasure and every pain, every friendship and every hatred, their sanctity, their good actions and the sinfulness of their bad actions as we see and know them in the providence of God in the Beatific Vision.

So we will know their lives, not as *they* experienced them in the 'time' they lived in, but in the all-creating power of God who made and directed them, in the all-complete knowledge of God, and in his personal and divine love for each of them. We will see how our lives affected them, and how their lives affected us. We will see how we have helped them and how they have helped us. We will know their sins, and they will know our sins — but we need not fear this! For we will know one another's sins as our loving and forgiving God does, and not with our sinful and limited human nature.

LITANY OF THE SAINTS (expanded)

Lord, have mercy on us   **Christ, have mercy on us.**
Lord, have mercy on us, Christ hear us
         Christ, graciously hear us.
God, the Father of heaven   **have mercy on us.**
God the Son, Redeemer of the world   **have mercy on us.**
God, the Holy Spirit   **have mercy on us.**
Holy Trinity, one God   **have mercy on us.**
Holy Mary   **pray for us sinners, now and at death.**
Holy Mother of God   *(repeat this response to the end)*
Holy virgin of virgins:
St Michael, Archangel,
         overcoming the power of Satan:
St Raphael, Archangel,
         sent by God to heal and protect his people:
St Gabriel, Archangel,
         telling Mary she was to bear the Son of God:
Blessed Adam and Eve, first parents of the human race,
         and first sinners to know God's forgiveness:
Blessed Abraham, chosen ancestor of Mary and Jesus,
         example of faith for all God's people:
Blessed Moses, holy leader who walked with God,
         you delivered God's people from captivity:
Blessed David, sinful king of God's people,
         singing psalms of praise and repentance to God:
Blessed Isaiah, prophet of God's people,
         foretelling the sufferings and death of Christ:
Saints Joachim and Anne, parents of Mary,
         showing the mother of Jesus what family life was:
St Joseph, husband of Mary,
         chosen to be head of the human family of Jesus:
St Zachary, faithful priest of God's temple,
         preparing John, your son, for the Spirit's call:
St Elizabeth, cousin of Mary, mother of John,
         inspired by the Spirit to sing Mary's praises:
St John the Baptist, last of the prophets,
         preparing people to welcome Jesus when he came:

Litany of the Saints

St Peter, repentant sinner, apostle and martyr,
                    first leader of Christ's church:
    (*Response* **pray for us sinners, now and at death**)
St Paul, grateful convert, apostle and martyr,
              proclaiming Christ's message to the gentiles:
St Andrew, Peter's brother, apostle and martyr,
              through whom Peter came to know Jesus:
St Matthew, tax-collector turned apostle,
              proclaiming Jesus in preaching and writing:
St Mark, missionary companion of Paul,
              writing the Gospel you heard through Peter:
St Luke, pagan convert, companion of Paul,
              evangelist and historian of early church life:
St John, youngest of the apostles,
              special friend of Jesus, Mary's protector:
St Thomas, apostle to India, martyr,
              strengthened in faith on seeing the risen Christ:
St Mary Magdalen, forgiven sinner,
              devotedly loving Jesus, your friend:
St Martha, careful housewife and saint,
              faithfully serving Jesus and his friends:
St James, apostle and martyr, first bishop of Jerusalem,
              explaining the duties of our daily life:
St Matthias, apostle appointed by human chance,
              chosen by Jesus to witness to his resurrection:
Saints Timothy and Titus, shepherds of God's people,
              faithfully following the guidelines of Paul:
St Simon, visitor from Cyrene,
              you helped Jesus, a stranger, carry his cross:
St Veronica, fearless in your kindness,
              you refreshed Jesus by wiping his face:
St Dismas, repentant at the moment of death,
              you heard Jesus promise you heaven:
St Stephen, deacon and first martyr of the Church,
              example to all who gave their lives for Christ:
St Laurence, deacon and martyr at Rome,
              following the example of Jesus in his sufferings:

St Cecilia, virgin and martyr of Rome,
                patron of church music and singing:
  (*Response* **pray for us sinners, now and at death**)
St Agatha, virgin and lover of Jesus,
                crowning a noble life with a martyr's death:
St Agnes, virgin and martyr, example of love,
                offering your young life for Christ's teaching:
Saints Perpetua and Felicity, virgins and martyrs,
                supporting one another in facing death for Jesus:
St Justin, philosopher, convert and martyr,
                defending the faith to the hour of your death:
St Athanasius, bishop and writer,
                proclaiming Jesus as true Son of God:
St Jerome, convert, priest and scholar,
                tirelessly defending and explaining the scriptures:
St Monica, holy wife and mother,
                converting husband by example and son by prayer:
St Augustine, repentant sinner, bishop and writer,
                defending truth and guiding us to holiness:
St Patrick, bishop and missionary from Britain,
                bringing Christ to the people of Ireland:
St Columban, Irish monk, scholar and missionary,
                renewing the Church in central Europe:
St Benedict, holy monk and spiritual leader,
                father and guide of the monastic life:
St Bede, priest, scholar and spiritual guide,
                teaching and praying to the moment of your death:
St Margaret, queen of Scotland,
                loving God as wife and mother:
St Bernard, renewing monastic life,
                working for peace and unity in the Church:
St Francis of Assisi, turning from a life of riches,
                you showed how to serve God by loving poverty:

St Dominic, priest, preacher and founder,
>defending the truth of the faith:
(*Response* **pray for us sinners, now and at death**)
St Anthony, gentle Franciscan,
>converting people who had lost the faith:
St Elizabeth of Hungary, queen, wife, mother, widow,
>personally caring for the sick and suffering:
St Thomas Aquinas, holy scholar and theologian,
>proclaiming Jesus in prayer and writing:
St Gertrude, holy scholar and philosopher,
>leading others to prayer by word and example:
St Frances of Rome, holy wife and mother,
>leading others to serve the sick poor:
St John of God, holy brother,
>founder of an order to serve the sick and needy:
St Catherine of Siena, learned Dominican tertiary,
>working for Christ in the world of your time:
St Thomas More, husband, father and martyr,
>defending Church teaching even to death:
St Ignatius Loyola, priest, founder of the Jesuits,
>leading people to follow Jesus in daily life:
St Francis Xavier, Jesuit priest and missionary,
>taking Christ's truth to peoples of the East:
St Jane Frances de Chantal, wife, mother and widow,
>founder of an order to help the poor and sick:
St Frances of Sales, bishop, writer, spiritual guide,
>renewing your people by zealous pastoral work:
St Vincent de Paul, priest and religious founder,
>working to renew the clergy and help the poor:
St Teresa of Avila, Carmelite nun and reformer,
>guide in the ways of mystical prayer:
St Martin de Porres, holy Dominican brother in Lima,
>using medicinal skills to help the sick poor:

St Philip Neri, working for youth and the sick poor,
> simple and joyful in your priestly service:
> (*Response* **pray for us sinners, now and at death**)

St Alphonsus Liguori, priest, scholar and founder,
> showing people the best way to live:

St John Vianney, parish priest of Ars,
> renewing your people in love by pastoral care:

St Peter Chanel, Marist missionary, priest, martyr,
> after your death, your people accepted Christ:

St John Bosco, priest and founder of an order
> to join in the work of educating youth:

St Pius 10th, Pope of early and frequent communion,
> working to restore all things in Christ:

St Charles Lwanga and companions, African martyrs,
> preferring death to an impure way of life:

St Bernadette of Lourdes, Mary appeared to you,
> to call sinful people to repentance:

St Therese of the child Jesus, young Carmelite nun,
> teaching your little way of child-like simplicity:

St Maria Goretti, child-martyr for chastity,
> devoted to God, you chose death rather than sin:

St Maximilian Kolbe, priest, missionary, publisher,
> you gave your life to save a fellow-prisoner:

All you our friends whom we knew in this life,
> and all you other millions whom we have not known:

All you saints who did not know the Catholic Church,
> you knew the mercy of Jesus, and died in his love:

All you saints who never knew Jesus in this life,
> whatever you did for one another, you did for Jesus:

Lamb of God, you take away the sins of the world
> ... **spare us, O Lord.**
> ... **graciously hear us, O Lord.**
> ... **have mercy on us.**

Let us pray: Father, we honour and imitate your saints whom you have taken to share your life in heaven, grant that our lives may become part of their joy, as they contemplate us in your providence and glory. We ask this through Christ, our Lord: **Amen**

REFLECTIONS ON DEATH

Purgatory

Note: Purgatory belongs to the 'next life', to 'life after death'. So it cannot be fully understood by our human minds, nor adequately expressed in human words. Our concepts and words are limited by our human experience, which in turn is confined to this present world of space and time. However, we have to think and speak about 'the next life', the life of God which Jesus promised we would share with him after death, and to do so we have to use human words. But we use these words 'analogically', with meanings different from the normal everyday meanings that relate to our present world of space and time. Unless we bear this in mind, we will find that we misunderstand much of the language that saints and scholars use to tell us about purgatory: they use words in analogical sense, and this applies especially to such seemingly simple, but very time-conditioned words as *before, after, until, first, then*.

In this world, we are usually oblivious of the hurt and suffering we cause to others by our sins, even our seemingly minor sins of unkindness and neglect. We never know it all. If we did, life here would probably become intolerable to us! But when we sometimes learn about, and perhaps have to watch and live with suffering we cause to someone we love, we can ourselves suffer real and human pangs of sorrow and regret. Remembering and reliving such moments of pain may help us to understand in some small way the pain we will surely experience after death, when we will know *all* this suffering, and know it in some way as God himself knows it — he who knows everything!

We will know not just the tiny part of such suffering that we were conscious of causing in the lives of the few people we knew, but all the suffering that resulted from our sins in the lives of thousands we never knew in this life, many who were not even born when we died.

I just cannot see God face to face, as he is in himself, as Jesus promised to those who love him, without knowing his complete plan and providence, including all the suffering that followed my sins in this world... all the suffering and pain undergone by other people at different moments of 'time' as a result of my sins... all the 'temporal suffering' (*poena temporalis*) that continues in this world even after my sin that caused it has been forgiven by my merciful Father... This will involve a big adjustment, a 'traumatic experience'.

And the adjustment will extend also to my learning how to love others as God loves them — especially people whom in this world I hurt, or refused to forgive, or despised, or neglected, or ignored, or merely disliked. I cannot even begin to love and enjoy God in heaven, and to share his life, unless I first learn to love everybody of this kind — each one of them, without any exception. This again will involve a big 'adjustment'.

And this adjustment, together with the adjustment of knowing for the first time, and learning to live with, our contribution to the world's suffering, must surely be a 'traumatic experience' that awaits us at the moment of death. Whether this will take place at a moment of time as we understand it in this life, or in the eternal 'moment' of the next life, we do not know… but for me, it clarifies at least one of the sufferings of purgatory, by which we will be purged and prepared for living our new life, our risen life, our divine life with Jesus Christ, sharing with him the inner hidden personal life of the Trinity.

Praying for the dead

When we learn of a death of a friend, or attend a funeral, we should follow the ancient Christian custom of praying for him or her, first commending his soul to God and asking God to take him to heaven, for God in his divine love is far more interested in having our friend with him in heaven. But we can also help our deceased friends in a real human way by assuring them, who hear us 'in God', that we forgive them for any hurt they may have caused us, that we accept all such hurt without passing it on to others, and that we will try to lessen by our prayers and good works, the hurts they have caused to others. And they are helped and made happy when they see us, again in God, thanking them for the help they gave us, being inspired to improve good living by their good example and our memories of them. When we pray for a dead friend, all our prayers, and even our very presence at a funeral, are known to our friend in the eternal 'now' of heaven, and contribute to that adjusting and purging that we call purgatory, which is a part of that new eternal life.

And this in turn, will help us to include all our dead in the first person plural of our prayers: 'pray for *us* sinners… forgive *us our* trespasses… deliver *us* from evil…' And 'all our dead' includes not merely those we knew in this life, but everybody in the world, those we know and do not know, those who died recently and those who died long ago, those who are listed in history books or newspapers and those who live quiet and unknown and forgotten lives in this world… And we should not forget the countless millions who will hear when they die the invitation: 'Come, you blessed of my Father, possess the kingdom prepared for you…', those countless millions who never knew Christ or his teaching in this life, and who therefore will have to ask, — as *we* will not have to ask — 'Lord, when did we see you hungry….'

Reflections on death

When a friend dies (Change pronoun if male)

Father, we praise your love for our friend (*name*),
whom through death, you called from this life of time.
Lord, in your love and mercy, look not on her sins,
but on the death of your Son, Jesus Christ,
which gives hope that she is one with him in heaven,
sharing with him in your life of the Trinity,
seeing you not dimly as in a mirror, but face to face,
knowing you as you really are,
and in you, knowing all things even as you know them.

In your eternal NOW, she sees your love and your care
and her place in the infinite beauty of your plan.
She sees why you loved her, and chose her for life.
She sees all human history in your eternal NOW,
with all the people she helped and who helped her.

She also sees every forgotten sin, every idle word.
In your forgiveness, she knows your mercy and love,
but she also sees how her wrongdoing hurt others,
all the bad example she gave, all the hurt she caused.
In her still human heart, she feels painful sympathy
for all the human suffering that followed her sins,
suffering of the past, of the present, of the future,
the pain she brought to people in our world of time,
the 'temporal suffering' due to her sins,
even the sins which you have already forgiven.

Lord, help her adjust to this painful experience
of seeing her sins and their effect on others
in the blinding light of your knowledge
and the burning flame of your love,
as she learns to see herself and her sins as you do.
Lord, tell her not to worry about any hurt done to us.
Let her see, in you, our love and forgiveness
and our acceptance of whatever suffering
you decide is our fair share of the world's suffering.
Let her see our thanks for her life and her love,
Let her hear, as you do, our promise to live for you,
as she sees us in your plan and loves us by your love.

Prayer for those in Purgatory

Father, you created us to live with you
and share with you the joy you have prepared for us,
which human eyes cannot see, nor human words explain,
in a new life, where a thousand years is like a day,
and the words 'before' and 'after' have new meanings
outside the time and space of this world.

At death, in the blinking of an eye,
you change our mortal life to an immortal life,
a life still the personal unique life of each of us,
though different to the life we had in this world,
as a plant is different to the seed it came from.

Lord, before we can live in the fullness of your joy,
we will stand before you to be judged,
and we must give an account of our whole life,
of faults forgotten until that first Day of eternity,
when the quality of our life on earth
is revealed to us in the light of your vision,
and is tested in the fire of your love.

We pray for those in purgatory, saddened and pained
by the evil of their sin they see living after them.
Let them see that the good they did also lives on,
and fits into your plan to bring people closer to you.

Comfort them also by showing them our love for them,
and how their lives and memories have helped us.
Comfort them, Lord, by letting them see in you,
how we try to sanctify the bad results of their sins,
and use them to bring holiness and joy to others,
through our love and acceptance and forgiveness,
as Adam sees his sin now called a 'blessed fault',
for it led Jesus to become man and die for us...
as David sees his sin, used in your saving providence
to bring into existence the ancestors of Jesus;
as the forgiven enemies of Jesus see their sins
turned on the cross into our redemption,
by the acceptance, forgiveness and love of Jesus.

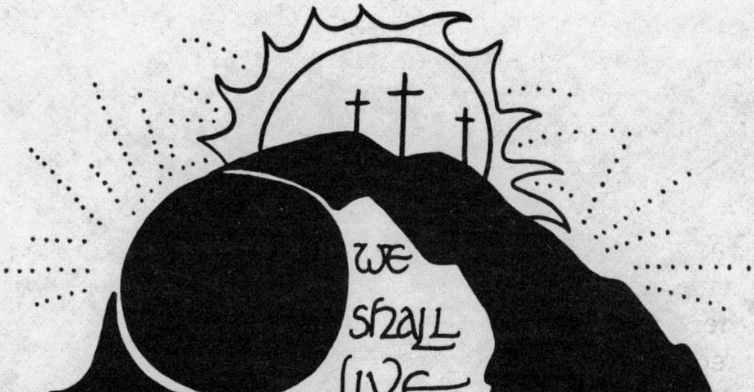
WE
SHALL
LIVE

Index

Introduction
praying	9
outline of Book	10
when and how to pray	12
additional Notes	14

The Presence of God
preliminary breathing exercise	17
God everywhere, God here	18
God in me	19
my creator's presence	20
my Father's care	21
an act of love	22

Living with Jesus, in the Father, by the Spirit
through, with and in Jesus	24
I pray to Jesus	25
the Jesus prayer	26
daily offering	26
the Name of Jesus	27
the Sacred Heart of Jesus	28
God, my Father, through Jesus	29
God, Spirit of love, sent by Father and Son	31
1001 prayers: explanation	32
1001 'Jesus prayers'	33
1001 prayers to God the Son	34
1001 prayers to God the Father	35
1001 prayers to God the Holy Spirit	36

Praying from the New Testament
history of the New Testament	37
the book of the Church	38
the New Testament today	39
personal prayer	40
praying with others — shared prayer	41
seven steps for shared meditation	41
group discussion	42
parish renewal scripture sharing	42

Our Daily Prayer

GUIDE TO NEW TESTAMENT PASSAGES

Life of Jesus from the Gospels

infancy	43
public life: actions and miracles	43
public life: teaching and parables	44
public life: saints and sinners	45
passion and death	46
the risen Christ	46
we live in Jesus. He lives in God	47

Holy Spirit sent by Father and Son

to make us holy	48
to explain vices, sin and repentance	48
to explain the duties of daily life	49
to help people doing God's work	49
to explain ministry and service	50
to explain holiness and virtues	50
to help the Church grow	51
to reveal God's plan to John	51

PRAYING WITH GOD'S PEOPLE

Psalms of David

temptation and suffering (from psalm 21)	52
trust in God's guidance (from psalm 142)	53
doing God's will (from psalm 39)	54
for help in old age (from psalm 70)	55
God hears and saves (from psalm 5)	56
praise God our creator (from psalm 26)	56
loving God (from psalm 15)	57
longing for God (from psalm 62)	57
for help against enemies (from psalm 30)	58
save me from sinfulness (from psalm 68)	59
God's knowledge and Law (from psalm 138)	60
praise of God's mercy (from psalm 85)	61
loving and praising God (from psalm 41)	62
mercy and praise (from psalm 56)	62
God's Law — my joy (psalm 118,2)	63
God's Law — my delight (psalm 118,3)	63
God's Law teaches me (psalm 118,9)	64
God's Law — my maker's instructions (psalm 118,10)	64
God's Law — my wisdom (psalm 118,13)	65
God's Law — my light (psalm 118,14)	65
God's Law shows his love (psalm 118,19)	66
God's Law protects me (psalm 118,20)	66
God's Law — my treasure (psalm 118,21)	67
God's Law — my support (psalm 118,22)	67

People of the Gospel

Zachary's prayer	68
the Angelus	69
Mary's Prayer: the Magnificat	69
petitions from the Lord's Prayer	70

Responding to Jesus' Last Supper talk

love and desire	71
knowing the Father	72
truth and peace	73
union with Jesus	74
glad to obey Jesus	75
sent to the world	76
guided by the Spirit	77
spreading the Good News	78
working for God	79

Responding to Epistles

the love of Christ	80
doing God's will	81
serving Jesus Christ	82
working for Jesus	83
God's loving plan	84
praising God's love	85
for God's people	86
God's plan for Jesus	87
loving our neighbour	88

Prayers of Saints

all things made through Jesus (Athanasius)	89
praising God (Augustine)	90
Augustine's resolution	91
changed by your love (Imitation of Christ)	92
loving the Lord (Imitation of Christ)	93
St Patrick's breastplate	94
hymn to Christ (Columba)	95
daily Prayer	96

THE BLESSED EUCHARIST

Reflections

'Do this in memory of me'	97
at Mass we offer our love to God	98
Mass is a sign of our love	99
Christ's love offered at Mass	100
four ways of loving God	100
bread and wine changed into Christ	101
we need faith to know the Mass	101

Mass offered by the double consecration	102
sharing the sacrificial feast	103
food of our souls	104
Mass ratifies our covenant	104
Mass is our offering for the Lord's day	105
we offer Mass together	106

Prayers before Mass

Christ is coming	107
act of love	108
knowing and loving God	109
proclaiming Christ's death	110
offering Christ's love	111
I offer myself	112

Prayers before communion

bread of life (John 6)	113
faith in your presence (Imitation of Christ)	114
prayer of desire	115
I am not worthy (Imitation of Christ)	116
I praise your love (Imitation of Christ)	117
Lord, forgive me (Imitation of Christ)	118
I need your love (Imitation of Christ)	119

Prayers after communion or after Mass

O Jesus, hidden God	120
food of the hungry	121
prayer of praise	122
humility and confidence	123
how I should love	124
holiness of life (Aquinas)	125
prayer of trust (Cardinal Newman)	126
for peace of heart (Cardinal Newman)	126
praying with Christ's friends	127

Prayers before the Blessed Sacrament

explanation	128
friendship and unity	129
offering Christ's love	130
prayer for others	131
trust, praise and peace	132
love and mercy	133
I praise God's love	134
sharing Christ's love	135
for the living and the dead	136
peace and unity	137
God of love and mercy	138
love and forgiveness	139

Index

example of Jesus	140
reconciliation	141
unity for your Church	142

THE SACRAMENT OF RECONCILIATION

introduction	143

Readings for confession

a sign bringing peace	144
vices, temptation and sin	145
confession. contrition	146
absolution. satisfaction	147
right living	148
holiness and sin	149

Prayers before confession

the soul's offering	150
acts of repentance from scripture	152
sin and mercy (Romans 1)	153
sinful desires (Romans 6,7)	154
devotion to God (Augustine)	155
Jerome's prayer for mercy	155
I live with Christ (from Romans 8)	156
Lord, have mercy (from 1 John 1,2)	157
prayer for pardon (Augustine)	158

Prayers after confession

our hope in Christ (from Romans 5)	159
to amend my life (from Romans 2)	160
free to serve others (from Galatians)	161
remaining faithful (from James 1)	162
false teachers (from 2 Peter 2)	163
love others (from 1 John 3)	164
St Gertrude's Resolution	165

THE SACRAMENT OF MARRIAGE

Prayers for married couples

married love (from Marriage Rite, blessings)	166
for husband and wife (from Marriage Rite, blessing)	167
prayer for my spouse (from Ephesians 5)	168
prayer of Tobias	170
love and marriage (from *Humanae Vitae*)	171
responsible parenthood (from *Humanae Vitae*)	172
love and children (from *Humanae Vitae*)	173
loving God in one another	174

DEVOTION TO OUR LADY

Praying the Mysteries of the Rosary
how to pray the rosary	175
praying the rosary well	175
the Hail Mary is a biblical prayer	176
response — Holy Mary	176
basis of the method	176
scripture readings	177
some phrases changed	177
group use	178
'blessed is Jesus'	178
a shorter rosary	179
singing the new version	179
repeating each phrase	179
conclusion	179
the Joyful Mysteries	180
the Sorrowful Mysteries	183
the Glorious Mysteries	186

Marian Devotions for Today: A Novena
introduction	189
opening prayer	190
we honour and love her	191
we call on her for help	197
we promise to imitate her	201

THE COMMUNION OF SAINTS

Reflections on the saints
how do the saints know us?	203
why do we pray to saints?	204
prayer to saints honours God	204
who are saints?	205
the saints are 'friends'	206
billions of friends!	207
Litany of the Saints	208

Reflections on Death
purgatory	213
praying for the dead	214

Prayers
when a friend dies	215
for those in purgatory	216